Mirror of Reality...

A Memoir

ROBIN DENISE BARNES

First Printing, Asta Publications, LLC, trade paperback edition
February 2015

Note to Readers
Names and identifying details of some persons portrayed in this book have been changed.

Library of Congress Control Number: 2014930460

ISBN 13: 978-1-934947-85-2

Manufactured in the United States of America

This Book is Dedicated With Love To:

My Parents

In loving Memory of my late father, William Robert Barnes. Thank you for your unconditional love, and for being the role models that epitomize greatness. Your faith in me is what kept me going; your belief in me gave me strength to keep fighting every time I wanted to give up. You are my heroes, and if I lived a thousand years; I could never repay you for all you've done for me, and my children. Words cannot express just how grateful, and blessed I am to have you as my parents. Thank you sincerely for loving me. Rest in peace Daddy, you were my trophy, and I am proud to call you my father. Words cannot express what your loss has done to me, but I can rest just knowing you're in a place of peace. I love you both… no one will ever fill your shoes.

My Sister

Mimi, you were not just my little sister; you were my best friend, and greatest inspiration. Your life brought substance to so many, and your death left a void that can never be filled. You've touched so many with your kindness; yet you stood your ground when you needed to. Your belief in me was instrumental in the completion of this book. You may be gone from this life; but never forgotten. I know you've found peace in the arms of God. I miss you every day, and love you immensely. There was so much left unsaid between us; but I believe you knew just how much I really loved you; but God loved you more, and for that reason he took you home to paradise. Rest in peace, I pray that I will see you again.

My Children

You are a product of the good that's inside of me. You've shown me your love, and respect even when I didn't deserve it. You each have a strength, and determination that I admire. I am blessed that God saw fit to allow me to be your mother, and through all the mistakes I've made in life; you are my greatest masterpiece, the one thing in life that I am most proud of. I love you.

My Grandchildren

You are the leaves of my tree, and one of the greatest gifts that God has given me. Your smile melts my heart, and your love brightens my soul. May you be blessed all the days of your life, and always know glam-ma loves you.

To My Siblings

We grew up together; sharing the same mother, and father. Yet we were all different, and unique. We've experienced happiness, and sadness together. We have memories that will last a lifetime, and no one can take that away. I love each of you, and I pray that your paths leads to a place of peace, and happiness.

My Extended Family

You are the added additions to my family. You are more than my son-in-law's, you're both my son's. Thank you for being the wonderful husbands and fathers to my daughters, and grandchildren. I love you.

Acknowledgments

The Bible says "faith without work is dead". Life's setbacks prolonged this book for its due season. I give all the honor, and the glory to my heavenly father who blessed me to still be alive to fulfill my purpose in life. God saw something in me that I didn't see in myself. I acknowledge God because his love is everlasting and I can do nothing without his grace, and mercy. I would also like to acknowledge the wonderful people in my life who believed in me, and supported me in this journey:

Derrick Smith, words cannot express just how much you mean to me. You believed in me; supported me, and inspired me to never give up, even when I wanted to. You are a valuable; priceless individual. You are truly a great friend! Thank you for loving, and having faith in me. I love you with all my heart!

Sandra Smith, you were the instrument God used to help me fulfill my dream. You opened your doors, and your heart to me and I will never forget it. You are not only a friend, you're my sister. Thank you for believing in me, motivating me and loving me.

Author Demetrias Dale Charles, thanks for your listening ear, and eagerness to lend a helping hand. Your wisdom, and guidance throughout this process was instrumental in the completion of this book. You are truly a wonderful friend, as well as a gifted; talented writer.

Assuanta Howard (ASTA Publications), this has been a long road and I want to thank you from the bottom of my heart for your warmth, and sincerity. I will be forever grateful. You helped me make a dream into a "Reality"

Louie @ Luv My Photo Photography, located in Riverside, California, thank you for the wonderful photo shoot and the beautiful picture that graces my book cover. You are awesome and your photos are amazing! Abman R. Glaster "Urban Legend Publishing" special thanks for designing my book cover, you did an amazing job and brought my cover to life.

My sister in spirit and best friend Alicia "Sister" Whitman, you have always made me feel that I could do anything! You stood by me through thick, and thin, and you believed in me no matter how farfetched my ideas were. Your love is a valuable asset to my life, and your friendship is priceless. My friend Richard Woods, we go a long way back, and have shared a lot of good times. Thank you for your input; guidance, and for walking me through this process. I don't know what I would have done without you!

My sister Tanijalyn R. Barnes, for being my best and worst critic, you always encouraged me to live my dreams, spread my wings, and fly. I love and respect your intelligence, and value your opinion. Thank you for reading my book, and pointing out my flaws, I expected nothing less from you.

My friend Gabrielle Bowden, Shawn Thornton, and my niece Ta'Merah Barnes, I want to thank you for reading the rough draft of my introduction; giving me your honest feedback, and a big thumbs up. You gave me the confidence I needed to push forward, and accomplish my dreams.

To everyone from my neighborhood 91st and Figueroa in South Central Los Angeles from 1966-present, you will always be my extended family. Judy, Catherine, Terry, Barbara and Lamont, just to name a few. We grew up together; we laughed, and cried together, and throughout life we remained friends. We have memories that will last a lifetime. I love you all very much.

Mable Oliphant, thank you for your beautiful spirit; for the joy, and love you spread that is so infectious. You are a light, and God shines in you. You brighten up my life with your honesty and unconditional love. Thank you for having unrelenting faith in my abilities.

To my cast of Character's, you know who you are. If it weren't for you, there'd be no me! I appreciate the lessons that I learned, and the memories; good and bad, because it taught me about myself. I have each of you to thank for my life experiences. You played a vital role in the person I am today. God bless you.

To my Facebook, Twitter and Instagram family, thank you for your support, and for hitting "Like" or giving your comments every time I wrote something about my book. Your continued support and encouragement gave me the strength I needed to reach my goal.

☩
Contents
☩

Contents

Preface

It's the spring of 2013, I can't believe the years have come and gone so quickly; life happened so fast, it seems as though it was just yesterday that I was eight years old lying in the front yard on the grass gazing into the sky asking God for a handful of grapes.

Fast forward forty-four years later and now it's two am and as usual I'm wide awake, staring up at the popcorn ceiling, whispering to God "please just let me die" because I just don't want to be here anymore.

No amount of alcohol or Xanax can help me sleep. I can't shut down my brain or stop the voices in my head from telling me just how much of a failure I am. Here I am age fifty-two; broken, penniless and homeless; sleeping on an air mattress on my friend's living room floor.

What happened to me? When did I give up on my life? The Bible says "God won't put more on you then you can bear" but I started to believe that couldn't possibly be true. Why did God think I was strong enough to carry such heavy burdens?

I've been told God has a purpose for everyone's life; well what's mine? I've failed at everything good that I've ever tried to accomplish, yet I succeeded at everything bad.

I'm tired of drinking, and taking pills to mask my pain. I had big dreams once; I was going to be a fashion designer, model and actress. I was going to travel the world, and do exciting things, rub elbows with the rich and famous. I was going to be somebody! I guess too many of Life's disappointments left me too afraid to try; for fear of failure.

I've been plagued with depression and alcoholism throughout the course of my life and I don't want to end up like my sister who drank herself to death at the age of thirty-nine, but I see myself headed in that direction. I find myself gazing in the mirror into eyes that look just like mine, and the reflection staring back at me is that of a stranger saying "Who are you?"

I guess the years of lying to myself and pretending to be some- one that I'm not have finally caught up with me.

As a child I wanted to be white, at age five I told my parents that I wasn't their child and that someday my real "White Parents" would come get me. I went as far as telling kids at school that I was adopted, because I was ashamed of being black.

At age six I watched my twenty-three year old pregnant mother have a massive stoke at a family barbecue on Father's Day in 1968 shortly after; I was molested, and physically abused by a babysitter at the age of seven.

Growing up poor, black and living in the ghetto of South Central Los Angeles didn't help much; with its Pimps, Prostitutes, Drugs addicts, and Gangs.

Don't get me wrong; I came from a good home, I had two loving parents' with morals, and values. My father worked two jobs, sometimes three, and they wanted nothing but the best for us.

However, nothing they did was ever good enough for me. I wanted more. I wanted what the white kids had. I didn't want to be poor; living in a rundown house in the ghetto getting eaten up by rats, and roaches.

It was in summer 1974 when my parents decided to voluntarily desegregate us. They sent us to a school two hours away from home because they wanted us to have the same education as the white children. I'm sure they thought they were doing what was best, but all it did was make me hate my life even more.

The white kids had nice houses; cars, and money. While we had nothing. The first day of school we were greeted with rocks and bottles thrown at the bus. It was then that I begin to hate being black, hate where I lived, and hate my parents for being poor!

At age fourteen my dreams of being a model, and actress were shattered when I was nearly burned to death in a freak accident at home.

At age sixteen unlike most of my friends, I was still a virgin playing with dolls; but my virginity was taken by a boy I knew; back then "no didn't mean no" I became a mother at sixteen. Well I had a baby; my mother became a mother and raised my child.

I managed to graduate high school, but it was hard. The kids were cruel and treated me like trash. They would whisper under their breath when I walked by; "that's the tramp that has a baby". All the boys thought I was easy, so I didn't date much. I managed to graduate high school, but it wasn't easy, and my life went from bad to worse.

At age nineteen baby number two came. I'd planned this one, because my boyfriend said he loved me, and promised to marry me. That dream faded when I found out he had another girl pregnant at the same time.

I was stuck with two kids; on welfare and food stamps. I had nothing and no one, so I drank, smoked cigarettes, and used drugs to hide the pain. I was an alcoholic by the age of nineteen.

Everyone thought I had it all together, but my life was a stage, and I put on a performance every day. I appeared to have it all on the surface; the looks, the body, and the confidence. But it was all an illusion.

At age fifty-two I find myself still searching for myself. The reflection staring back at me in the mirror is that of a lost soul, beaten up by life without a pot to piss in or a window to throw it out of.

I guess it's time to separate fantasy from reality, after all I've got less time in front of me than I do behind me, and at the rate I'm going I won't be here much longer.

The stress of life's disappointments, and failures has chewed me up and spit me out, like a piece of old meat stuck in your teeth. It seemed no matter how hard I tried happiness and success wasn't in the cards for me.

The Eighties came, and that's when Crack Cocaine hit the streets of South Central Los Angeles hard, most of the girls I grew up with were dating drug dealers; being wined and dined and given fancy cars and shopping sprees, but not me, I wasn't good enough.

My self-esteem was so low that the only men I attracted were the liars, cheaters, and abusers. I was starving for love, but every man in my life was toxic; like a chronic disease that infected my body and destroyed my spirit, none of them cared about me, or what I'd been through. I accepted them because I felt worthless, and having someone was better than no one at all.

I suffered physical abuse at the hands of almost every man I'd ever loved or thought I loved; I had as many broken bones as I had broken dreams, and as time went on I had given up on ever finding someone to love me. I realized I didn't love myself so how could I expect anyone else to love me.

I was tired of struggling; I wanted more out of life than just food stamps and a welfare check. I was living below the poverty level. I could barely afford clothes, and shoes for myself, and my two children. Four hundred, and twenty-seven dollars a month didn't go far, and I couldn't make ends meet so that's when I decided to start selling drugs.

At age twenty I left my kids with my parents; it wasn't like I was much of a mother, or played a significant role in their life anyway. I set out on a journey for fortune, and fame which would ultimately lead to my self-destruction. This decision nearly cost me my life.

I worked my way up in the drug world. I went from selling crack on the street corner, and being a mule (carrying drugs on airplanes) to being named the leader, and organizer of a drug distribution ring by the age of twenty-six.

That lifestyle came at a cost and a few years later I found myself charged with seventeen counts of conspiracy; facing twenty-five years to life. I thought going to prison was my rock bottom, but I was wrong! That was just the tip of the iceberg.

I was beaten up by life so bad I attempted suicide a few times, but God wouldn't let me die. I couldn't even kill myself right. I searched high and low for myself, but I couldn't find me.

No amount of money, drugs or alcohol could help me forget the countless mistakes I'd made. I burdened my poor mother, and father with the responsibility of raising my children. I couldn't get high enough to forget that I treated my kids like all the men in my life treated me; as though they were nothing!

When I wasn't making a mess of my life; I spent a majority of it in hospitals fighting for my life. The doctor's gave me a death sentence several times, but that wasn't in God's plan either.

I spent years mad at God, my parents, and all the men who'd ever hurt me. I blamed them for my terrible life. It wasn't until I took a long look in the mirror; not at the image looking back at me, but into the soul of the woman staring back at me. I realized I had no one else to blame for my dreadful life and poor choices, but myself. I gave up; I accepted defeat.

I spoke negative things into the universe, and snared my own success. I finally realized I had to stop playing the victim. I asked God to show me myself, and when he did; I had to repent, and forgive myself for all the wrong I'd done. Then I had to forgive everyone who'd ever hurt me, and ask for forgiveness from everyone I'd hurt, but that isn't easy. I want to die guilt free with no regrets, and I know I have a long road ahead of me, but I'm determined to succeed this time.

Chapter One

A Fighter was Born

A solar eclipse occurred; blocking all direct sunlight, turning the day into darkness on February 5, 1962. This was the day I almost died being born!

It was a cold, dreary day when my mother went into labor. When mama gave birth to me I was very ill, and had to have several blood transfusions; the doctors feared I wouldn't survive. Mama said I looked like a dried up little bird so she named me Raven.

My introduction into this world was a sheer indication of what my life was going to be, an uphill fight for survival.

I had two loving parents, and four siblings, three sisters and a brother. My Daddy was born in Brookhaven, Mississippi, and was an only child of an only child so his side of the family was very small. It consisted of Him, his mother Emma, and his grandmother Mary.

My dad was a handsome man; he wasn't very tall about 5'9, with chocolate colored skin; black hair, and brown eyes.

He had a charming smile, and Pearly white teeth. He was an athlete that played sports in high school, and college until he joined the navy.

Mama was born in Baton Rouge, Louisiana; she had three sisters, and three brothers. Mama was bi-racial; her mother was half white, and her father was Indian and black.

Mama was gorgeous; she had cold black hair that she kept cut short, a big vibrant smile, beautiful brown almond shaped eyes, and caramel colored skin. She was petite standing at only 5' 4.

Mama didn't graduate high school; she dropped out in the eleventh grade because she became pregnant with my sister Tina. My parents married when mama was just sixteen, and daddy was eighteen.

My parents moved to California when I was three. My father was a cook, and a dishwasher. He managed to take care of a family of seven making only eight dollars an hour. Sometimes he would work two or three jobs at a time just to make ends meet.

Daddy always kept a roof over our head; food on the table, and clothes on our backs. We lived in a small duplex, located in South Central Los Angeles, near a popular street called Figueroa. It was known for its Pimps, Prostitutes, Drug addicts, and Drunks.

I can't leave out the "Crips" they were the local gang that took over our streets, and thought they owned it. They instilled fear in everyone living in the neighborhood while bringing everybody's property value down with their gang violence.

None of them owned anything yet they claimed areas of Los Angeles as their territory, and had the people who did own their homes scared to walk the streets.

We lived between an alley, and a freeway. There was a dope house next door, where most of the prostitutes had sex, and drug addicts hung out to shoot up their heroin. It was normal to see a pimp beating up one of the prostitutes, or drug addict overdosing in the alley.

There were drunks standing on every corner, but they were harmless most of the time. I'm sure if Daddy could afford a better place for us to live he would have.

Mama was a house wife, and by the time she was twenty-one she already had four kids. Mama had lots of friends; who spent the majority of the time at our house, smoking cigarettes, drinking and listening to music while Daddy was at work. This was something we became accustom to.

As early as the age of four I could remember sneaking in the living room so I could steal sips from their beer cans when they weren't looking. This is probably why I became an Alcoholic by the age of nineteen.

I remember one day Daddy came home after a hard day's work to a house full of people. Daddy didn't socialize much and didn't have many friends; unlike Mama. They say opposites attract, and they were right.

Mama and Daddy were like night and day. He was quiet and stayed to himself; she was out spoken and loved to be surrounded by people. I guess it came from their different upbringing: him being an only child and her coming from a large family.

Daddy walked in the house, grunted hello to everyone and headed straight to his bedroom; closing the door behind him.

Mama was playing a record by Aretha Franklin called "Respect." She played it over, and over until finally Daddy (who was never much for words unless he had some liquor in him) came out of the room; picked up the stereo, and threw it on the floor without saying a word. He calmly walked back to his bedroom; closed the door, and at that point the party was over!

I thought daddy was mean because he didn't like to have fun, but he was a family man and the only thing that mattered to him was his wife and children. He didn't have a lot of friends and it seemed as though that's the way he preferred it.

Daddy never knew his biological father. He'd left the picture long before Daddy was born. His mother married a man name Jesse, and he grew to love my father, and adopted him when he was seven. They became very close. Jesse would take daddy fishing on the weekends so he could spend time with him alone.

Tragically that all came to an end one weekend when Jesse went on a fishing trip alone. The boat capsized; he fell into the water, hit his head, and drowned. Daddy was fourteen years old at the time.

For years he felt guilty over his father's death. He believed if he had been there maybe he could have saved him. When daddy shared that story with me I could see the hurt in his eyes even after all those years.

Daddy wasn't affectionate, and didn't show much emotion. We knew he loved us by the things he did for us. Every time we'd say "I love you" he'd say "me too". As a child I didn't understand why he never said the words "I love you" but as I got older I realized what "me too" meant.

Daddy worked six days a week; sometimes sixteen hours a day. He made sure we had clothes on our backs, and shoes on our feet, even if it meant he only had one pair of worn out shoes with holes in them for himself. He rarely brought anything for himself, but he always made sure we were taken care of.

No matter how hard times were Daddy always managed to get us something for Christmas and our birthdays. He saved for an entire year just to take us to Disneyland and whatever he was determined to do he did it.

I know it must have been a struggle trying to provide for a wife, and five children, but somehow daddy made it look easy and he never complained.

Daddy never quit at anything, and he didn't do to us what his biological father had done to him, which was leave us.

I always sensed a deep sadness in my father, but he never let us into his head, or told us how he really felt. He kept everything bottled up inside, and I guess I inherited that gene to.

I always wanted a man like my father. He loved, and adored my mother. He was loyal, and devoted. He stood by her side no matter what, and that meant the world to me. As I grew older I began to realize they just didn't make men like him anymore.

Daddy was never much for words, so on the rare occasion that I did get to talk to him, I'd find him sitting in front of the Television watching the Lakers play basketball, and drinking a beer.

Daddy didn't drink much, but when he did; he'd talk to us more than usual. He always said the same thing, "the white man ain't gonna give you a damn thing, you gotta get an education if you want to get anywhere in this world".

My sisters and I would laugh, and whisper behind his back because we thought he was drunk; but it turns out daddy knew what he was talking about, and he was right most of the time.

Mama was a nurturer. She was very loving, and caring, and made a point of always telling us how much she loved us. She was very affectionate, and always hugged, and kissed us.

I always wanted to be her favorite, so I always competed for her attention, and affection. Mama always said she didn't have any favorites, but I always felt that she favored all of my siblings over me.

I remember when I was in the sixth grade it was report card day and I was so excited to show mama my grades. I ran all the way home because I had all A's.

When I burst through the door my sisters were surrounding mama. We all took turns showing her our report cards, and I wanted to be last so I could really surprise her. Each time my sisters gave her their report cards she hugged and kissed them and told them how proud she was.

My heart was racing with excitement and I could barely wait for her reaction. I just knew mama was gonna praise me for my excellent grades, but when it was finally my turn she looked at my report card, and said "Oh Raven, I knew you would do well". I was heartbroken. I couldn't believe that's all mama said. I started to think I did it all for nothing. Maybe if I got bad grades mama would pay more attention to me too.

Everyone always said I resembled her the most, and I was proud of that. She was the most beautiful women in the world to me. Mama had a way of making me laugh after she had just whooped me, and made me cry.

Although she was young; she was no joke, and she didn't take any crap off of us. She had rules, and if we broke them, she didn't have a problem getting an extension cord, hot wheel track or anything else she could get her hands on to beat the fear of God into us.

When I was eleven years old I got in trouble for cussing at school. When I got home Mama told me she was going to whoop me. She sent me outside to get a switch off the big tree that sat in our front yard.

I searched that tree high, and low until I found a tiny limp branch and handed it to her. She looked at me with the stare of death, and if looks could kill; I would have dropped dead on the spot.

I knew I had to make a run for it, so I ran as fast as I could, and hid under the bed. Just when I thought I'd escaped, there she was standing over the bed telling me to come out.

My heart was pounding so hard I could see it beating through my shirt. I knew what was coming next. Of course I didn't come from under the bed willingly, and that just made matters worse. I thought she would get tired of yelling and leave, but that was far from what happened.

Although she could only use her right arm; mama had super human strength. She lifted the mattress, box spring and all, which I was clinging to for dear life with such force that it ended up leaning against the wall.

Mama peeled me off the box spring like a fruit roll-up, and I got one of the worse whooping's of my life. I always feared Mama, and from that day on when it was time to get punished I'd beg her to let Daddy do it, because he had mercy on me.

At a young age we were taught how to cook, and clean. Heaven forbid if we left a dirty dish in the sink! Mama would wake us all up in the middle of the night; it didn't matter what time it was or if we had to go to school the next morning or not.

She would take all the dishes out of the cabinets, and make us wash every single one of them. That was the punishment for not making sure the kitchen was clean before we went to bed.

We didn't have much; our roof leaked, and the side door to our house didn't close completely. We had to shove a butter knife in it at night to keep it shut, and even though we lived in the ghetto I still felt safe.

My parents brought the old dilapidated duplex in hopes of converting it into a single family home, and for a short time all seven of us lived on one side of the twelve hundred square foot house with two bedrooms and one bathroom on one side.

Daddy planned to hire someone to open the wall between the two units so we could have more space. A year had past, and he still didn't have the money to do it.

One day out of the blue mama took it upon herself to get a sledge hammer, and knock down the wall all by herself. Daddy came home from work to a house with a gigantic hole in the wall. The floor was covered in water, concrete and dirt, because mama hit a water pipe during the demolition.

Our house sat next to an alley, and the rodents would crawl in through holes in our roof. I dreaded the rain because the roof would leak. Once when my sisters and I were asleep a rat got in, and bit me on my lip. To make matters worse the ceiling fell on me the same night!

Daddy did his best to patch up the roof, and Mama did her best to keep the rats and roaches out, but their attempts were futile.

Mama said the rats and roaches were coming from the alley, and the filthy neighbor next door. She put poison around the house to try to keep them out, but the stray cats and dogs would eat it and die so Mama stopped doing that.

Our house was very clean considering there were five children living in it. And although we never owned a piece of furniture that wasn't used, or a new car. Mama and Daddy were grateful and took good care of everything we had.

Sometimes Mama would even shop at the thrift store for our school clothes. I despised wearing someone's used clothes; the thought of it made my skin crawl. I would cry every time she took us to the Goodwill, because I didn't like the smell of the old worn out clothes and shoes. I would beg her not to buy me anything, because I'd rather have nothing than someone's used hand me downs.

I always felt different from my sisters; like I didn't belong in our family. I couldn't sleep on the old sheets that we had if there were any stains on them, because it would make me itch. I'd get the biggest bath towel I could find, and lay it over the sheets. I'd ball up like an embryo, and make sure not to let any part of my body touch the sheets.

I did the same thing in the old rusty bath tub. The thought of my feet touching the bottom of that nasty tub made me cringe. I would often get in trouble for wasting the "good" towels, but I didn't care how many whooping's I endured. I just couldn't imagine my body touching anything dirty.

Mama tried to understand me, and sometimes she'd save a good towel just for me so I could sleep at night. In hindsight the tub wasn't really dirty, it was just a little rust around the drain, but in my five year old mind it was disgusting.

My parents wanted us to appreciate what we had, and to take pride in it. We couldn't leave the house until our beds were made, floors were swept, and dishes were washed.

Mama was firm, and when she took us anywhere we knew to sit down right next to her and not ask for anything. If we were hungry, thirsty or had to use the bathroom we were to sit quietly, and wait until Mama gave us permission.

We were taught to say yes sir, no sir, yes mam and no mam, and we were never to address an adult by their first name. I use to think that was slave talk, but dare I say anything to mama for fear of getting slapped in the mouth.

My sisters all knew not to question mama or daddy about anything, but not me. I always needed an answer, which caused me to get it trouble all the time; because I couldn't keep my big mouth shut.

Whenever one of us did something we weren't supposed to do; mama would round us up like a herd of cattle from the oldest to the youngest. We would stand there from oldest to youngest; like we were in a police lineup awaiting our fate.

I wasn't going down for something I didn't do, and I had no problem telling mama I didn't do it, My sisters stood there silent and took their whooping without a fight, but I made a run for it every chance I got; because I knew mama couldn't catch me.

Once I ran in the back yard, climbed a six foot brick fence and sat there for hours. Finally daddy came home and got me down. I could barely walk, and my butt was numb. I thought I got away home free, but mama waited until I got out the bath tub, naked and beat the mess out of me with a braided switch.

I always thought different from my sisters, they keep quiet no matter what, innocent or guilty they took their punishment without uttering a word. I was out spoken and whatever came to mind I would say it. I didn't know how to filter my words which often meant me getting in trouble.

I used to think Mama was mean, but I realized she was teaching us manners, and etiquette. Something most of the kids in our neighborhood knew nothing about.

Mama was an optimist, she tried to shelter us from the world. Mama never even taught me about the birds and the bees because she thought that was too much information. She wanted us to see only the good in people and to trust God for everything.

Daddy was a pessimist he never sugar coated anything and tried his best to prepare us for the cold cruel world. They both taught us to be thankful for everything we had and for a brief moment in time I was.

At age six my life took a turn for the worst. It was Father's Day 1968. My sisters and I were at a barbeque with our parents. We were in the backyard playing when suddenly I heard screaming, and shouting and saw people running.

We weren't allowed back in the house, so we peeked through the window and I saw my twenty-three year old pregnant mother lying on the floor motionless.

I could hear the other kids whispering "their mother is dead" finally one of the grown-ups came outside and gathered us together, and told us our mother was taken to the hospital.

Little did I know that would be the last time I'd see mama normal again. My sister's, and I sat together hugging each other, and crying. We didn't know what was to become of our mother. It would be a long time before we would see her again.

We were later told that she suffered a massive stroke; a blood clot ruptured on her brain. The doctors held little hope that she would survive. I overheard daddy tell my grandmother the doctors said that if mama survived she'd be a vegetable.

I couldn't understand how Mama could turn into a vegetable from being sick, and Daddy never explained that to me. I kept wondering what kind of vegetable Mama would turn into, and what would happen to my little brother or sister. That was the first time I'd ever seen my father cry, but it wouldn't be the last.

My grandmothers' and my great grandmother took turns coming out to California from Louisiana to help take care of us. It was hard for everybody. My father worked two jobs, and when he wasn't working he was at the hospital by mama's bedside.

Daddy purchased this beat up, old car that we would all squeeze into. We called it the "gold car" because it was the color of a solid gold bar. It wasn't much to look at, but it got us around; at least sometimes anyway. Just when he was about to make the last payment, somebody stole the car from in front of our house.

Daddy had it hard, but he never complained! To make matters worse one day he slipped, and fell at work, and broke his foot, he had to hop miles to the bus stop with a heavy cast on his leg, and crutches. He had to take three buses just to get to work and he never missed a day.

Sometimes Daddy would come home from work in so much pain,

his feet would be swollen. I guess it was from standing for sixteen hours a day. My sisters and I fill a bucket with hot water and Epsom salt so he could soak them. His back hurt so bad that he would crawl down on the floor, and my sisters, and I would take turns walking on his back.

He had calluses on his hands from washing dishes, and burns on his arms from cooking. No matter how much pain he was in; he never missed a day at work, or the hospital to see Mama.

The day had finally come when they moved Mama from intensive care to the Rehabilitation Center. It would be the first time we would get to see Mama since she had the stroke. I was nervous and excited, I couldn't wait to see Mama and tell her everything that I had done at school, and show her that I knew how to comb my own hair.

When we arrived at the hospital Daddy sat us all down, and calmly told us to be prepared. He said "your mama ain't the same anymore". I didn't quite understand what he was trying to say, but the memory of that day has been embedded in my mind ever since.

As we walked into the dimly lit room with its pale green walls; I could see and hear other patients moaning and groaning in pain, and I could smell the odor of feces and urine as I looked around impatiently for mama.

I couldn't believe the vision that sat before me. My once beautiful, vibrant mother was now bald, her mouth twisted to one side. She couldn't speak, and was slumped over in a wheel chair with her left arm curled up next to her side.

I stood there frozen; staring at her, trying to comprehend who this woman was. The tears began rolling down my face as I thought to myself; this is not my mother! My sisters ran over and hugged her, but I just couldn't. I just stood there in a daze wondering; what happened to my mother?

The ride home that day was quiet, and for the first time in my life, I had nothing to say. That was the beginning of the end of my seemingly normal life. Little did I know my life was about to get worse.

Chapter Two

Robbed of Innocence

It was now the summer of 1969; it had been a year since Mama had the stroke, and was hospitalized. My grandmothers had gone back to Louisiana, and we were sent to stay with my Aunt Catherine. She was my favorite Aunt because she was always nice to me; besides I didn't really know my other Aunts because they lived in Louisiana.

She was quiet, and soft spoken. She talked proper English, and used big words. Her kids talked the same way; so we would tease them, and call them Uncle Tom's, because they spoke like white people. Aunt Catherine was Mama's oldest sister. She had three kids, a daughter Patricia, and two sons Raymond and Timothy.

I was now seven, and I was excited to go visit my cousins because they were the only relatives we had in California. They lived in a City called Perris. It was hours away from South Central; at least that's how long it took us to get there when Daddy drove. Daddy didn't like to drive fast, and every time he drove it took us a long time to reach our destination.

Mama was a different story. Daddy said she had lead feet because she drove so fast. I didn't understand what that meant at the time; all I knew was Mama would always tell us to sit back in our seats, and when she drove we always got wherever we were going a lot quicker.

My cousins called Perris the good part of town, because there were no pimps, prostitutes or drugs addicts in their neighborhood. Daddy sent us there for the summer while he worked. My aunt always bragged about how peaceful it was where she lived; she said there was no crime, and that it was much safer than the city.

My Aunt Catherine lived near a farm where there were stinky pigs; chickens, and roosters. It didn't smell better than the city, but it was a far cry from South Central Los Angeles. It looked like the desert; there weren't many houses, and it was very hot. There were mountains surrounding us everywhere, and it looked nothing like where we lived, it was desolate, with tumbleweeds rolling down the dirt roads, and the few houses that were there didn't even have grass. There were no liquor stores, or motels on every corner where they lived. I just knew we were going to have a good time. Whenever my cousins came to visit us we always had fun. I couldn't wait to spend time with my Aunt, because she was the closest thing to a mother that I had since mama got sick, and went away.

We weren't even in the door good when she started telling us the rules. I thought Mama was precise, but she was nothing compared to Aunt Catherine. She had so many instructions she had them written down, and plastered on the refrigerator.

We weren't allowed to touch the walls, or lean on them, because she said they were weak. We weren't allowed to open the refrigerator even to get a drink of water. All the food was marked with the words "do not touch" to ensure we didn't eat it. She even drew a black line with a water proof marker on the water jugs, and milk.

It seemed to me as though she didn't really want us there. This was not the Aunt I remembered when she came to visit us. It was times like this that I really missed Mama. Although my Aunt wasn't very affectionate like our mother, we knew she loved us in her own funny sort of way.

My sisters, and I were all around the same age as Patricia, and her brothers, and we very close; like sisters and brothers.

It was the weekend when we arrived, so we played outside all day in the hot ninety degree heat, and at night we would make pallets on the floor with our blanks, and tell ghost stories.

My cousin Patricia would sneak anything she could find out of the kitchen for us to eat, because my Aunt didn't feed us enough. I don't think she did it on purpose; I just think she didn't have enough to feed us all, so she divided what she had between all seven of us.

My cousins all had their own rooms; which was something we didn't have. I wished for the day I could have my own room and sleep in my own bed. The thought of having some privacy, and a place to put my things away instead of hiding everything under the bed was something I longed for.

My cousin Patricia didn't seem to mind sharing her room, or her toys. It was as though having her own space meant nothing to her. She didn't have to share her clothes, toys or bed with anyone unlike me, and I was jealous.

Deep inside I wished I could trade places with her, and have her life. I thought she was lucky, but she was just happy to have us there to keep her company.

My Aunt hired a babysitter to take care of us while she worked. Her name was Eula, and I'll never forget her. She must have been about nineteen or twenty years old. She was a tall, skinny, black girl with short nappy hair, and long pointy chin like a witch.

Eula had teeth the color of mustard, and she didn't look as though she took a bath, because her feet were always dirty! Eula came in, flopped down on the couch, light up a cigarette, and began to yell, and curse at us.

The first day she started I could tell she didn't like me. When she looked at me she had an evil look in her eyes like the devil. I knew how the devil looked from my constant nightmares. Ever since mama left I had them, and each night they were almost identical. Every time I tried to tell Eula something she'd shew me away like a fly.

She would barely feed us, sometimes we would steal food, and hide to eat it. If she caught us; she'd hit us, or throw us outside in the scorching heat. There was no shade outside for us to take cover, because there were no trees, so we would turn on the water hose if we were thirsty, or too hot; just to cool off.

As time passed, Eula began locking me in the house. She'd lock the rest of the kids outside, and then physically abuse me for no reason. Some days were worse than others. At first it was just a slap in the face, a punch, or a kick. Then it progressed to sexual abuse.

She made me touch her breasts, and put my mouth on them. She would tell me to suck them like I was sucking a bottle. She would play in my vagina with her fingers, and put her mouth on my private area.

She kissed me in my mouth like a man kisses his wife. Her tongue tasted of stale cigarettes. I knew all too well what stale cigarettes tasted like, because I had stolen one of Mama's once, and tried to smoke it in the back yard. It left a nasty taste in my mouth, and made me choke.

I couldn't understand why this was happening to me. Although I was only a mere seven years old, I knew girls were supposed to kiss boys. I saw that on television, and at the drive-in when mama, and daddy took us to see "Claudine". We were supposed to cover our eyes on the grow-up parts but I always peeked.

I kept saying to myself, I'm a girl, and she's a girl", why is she doing this to me? I was confused, and Eula put the fear of God in me, and made me swear that I wouldn't tell anyone what she was doing to me.

I was afraid she would really hurt me, so I kept quiet for a while. I started having nightmares about Eula when I went to sleep, and it was worse than dreaming about the devil. I dreaded going to sleep at night, fearing what she was going to do to me next day.

One day I told Eula I was thirsty. She gave me this annoyed look; then got up slowly, walked into the kitchen, and got a cup of hot water from the sink. I watched as she put her cigarette butt in it, and forced me to drink it. Sometimes she would use me like an ash tray, and burn me in the palms of my hands just for fun.

I endured her torment for what seemed to be an eternity. In reality it was only a few weeks. I was afraid to tell my aunt, because I didn't think she'd believe me anyway. The consequences of that were too great, because if she told Eula she would deny it, and then she might do the things she threatened to do to me.

As the torture grew worse I eventually confided in my sister Tina, and my cousin Patricia. I made them promise not to say anything to anyone. They kept my secret, and at night we would all huddle together, and pray that Eula would die or just disappear, and never come back again.

It seemed the longer I kept silent, the worst the torment Eula inflicted on me became. Things got so bad that we came up with a plan to get rid of her. That night we left a window cracked open in Patricia's bedroom, so if she tried anything they'd climb in and stop her. We didn't know how we were going to do it, we just knew we had to do something.

The next morning she fed us breakfast, and told everyone but me to go outside, and play. She locked me in the house, and begin physically, and sexually abusing me. This time was worse than all the others. She hit me with a belt, and tried to put objects inside my vagina. I cried, and screamed as loud as I could, she got on top of me, and covered my mouth with her hand.

I bit her as hard as I could, and when she moved her hand I screamed as loud as I could. I could see my sister Tina watching through a small opening in the curtains. My cousin Timothy climbed through the window, and unlocked the back door. They all ran in and ambushed her.

They all began throwing anything they could get their hands on to get her off of me. They were hitting her with shoes, and kicking her. Then all seven of us; ages five through nine jumped her! We punched; slapped, and bit her, and when she finally broke free, she went running for the front door leaving her purse, and cigarettes behind, and that was the last we ever saw of Eula!

When we told our Aunt what happened but she didn't believe us. She thought we made the story up because we didn't like her.

That night my Aunt called daddy, and he came to get us the next day.Soon we were back home in the safety of South Central Los Angeles, and ironically I felt safe again.

I didn't know just how damaging Eula's violence and sexual abuse had affected me, but mentally and emotionally I was not the same. The happy go lucky seven year old that went to visit was gone, and the seven year old that came back saw life through a different set of eyes.

My innocence was taken in the blink of an eye I didn't think, or feel like a little girl anymore. When I came home I wasn't the same. I would beat my dolls, and then make them have sex. The thoughts that raced through my mind were not those of an innocent child, and I couldn't make them stop.

I didn't have anyone to talk to; Mama was still in the hospital, and Daddy was working all the time. I tried to divulge my feelings to Tina, but she just told me was to try to forget about it, so I stopped talking about it, and began living in my fantasy world. It was a place no one could imagine, but me.

In my world, I was a rich white girl. I had everything I wanted. A big fancy mansion, lots of beautiful clothes, and my own bedroom. I was an only child, and my parents adored me.

I would spend hours in the back yard alone in this little shack that I pretended was my castle. I would make clothes for myself out of rags, and sit outside until the street lights came on. Daddy would have to make me come inside.

My thoughts were not the same anymore. I had immoral visions, and fantasies about girls. I looked at them in a sexual way. I tried to get those thoughts out of my head, but they just wouldn't go away.

I'd wake up in the middle of the night in a cold sweat, crying uncontrollably still haunted by Eula. Most of the time she would be chasing me, trying to make me do bad things in my dreams.

I never felt safe even though I slept in bed with my two sisters, I would make sure to lay very close to them every night, and if I couldn't feel their legs, or feet in the bed, I'd wake up in a panic; afraid I was alone.

Most of the time I would toss, and turn all night; afraid of dreaming. Sometimes I'd fall asleep at school, and the teacher would send me to the principal's office. When he'd asked me what was wrong; I'd lie because I was ashamed to tell him what happened to me.

I kept my feelings inside, because that's all I knew how to do. I didn't know what people would think or say about me if I ever told them the truth, so I went on throughout my childhood hiding my pain se, and baring my secret.

Chapter Three

The Little Church on the Corner

One Sunday morning I heard a knock at the door; I ran to get Daddy because we were told never to open the door for strangers, or the Jehovah witnesses, because they would come by early in the morning to give a sermon, or had out pamphlets.

When Daddy opened the door to my surprise, there stood an elderly couple holding a plate of cookies. The man was short, and thin with fine black hair. He looked as though he was white, but he was creole. The lady was a short, chubby black woman, with dimples in both cheeks, a smile that could light up any room, and one of the sweetest voices I had ever heard.

They introduced themselves as Elder and Mother Stevens. They informed Daddy that they had just opened a church across the street, and asked if we could come on Sunday.

Daddy explained that Mama was in the hospital, and that he needed help to comb our hair, and get us dressed. The lady gladly agreed to come over, and help. They gave each of us two cookies, a big hug, and went on their way.

We were not a very religious family. I remember only going to church a few times on Easter, and Christmas, but for the most part we didn't attend church often.

That next Sunday Mother Stevens came over to help comb our hair, and get us ready for church. Somehow daddy figured out a way to get out of going, so my sisters and I anxiously walked across the street hand in hand to the little Pentecostal church.

The church sat on the corner of Figueroa and 91st place; next to the Chinese cleaners and adjacent to the Hacienda Motel where the singer Sam Cooke was murdered.

The church was shaped like a box. It couldn't have been more the

500 square feet. It had a tiny little bathroom, an office and a room in the back of the church with a baptism pool.

There weren't many members, and it wasn't very big, but you could feel the love. The members greeted us with hugs, and kisses just like Mama always had.

After all the hurt, and pain I endured at such a young age; I gravitated to it. From that day on I couldn't wait to go to the little church on the corner, so I could get my macaroon cookie; which was stale most of the time, and my cup of punch.

The church was very strict. We weren't allowed to wear pants or short skirts. We couldn't listen to any music that wasn't gospel. We were taught that the world was going to come to an end, and that if we didn't get saved we would burn in hell for eternity.

Everyone had to get the Holy Ghost, and speak "in tongues" to get to heaven. This was the language only God understood. I tried my best to get saved, and speak in tongues, so I could get the Holy Ghost, and go to heaven in the rapture.

Hell didn't sound as if it was a very fun place to end up, and after spending the summer at my Aunt's house, I didn't like the heat, so I definitely didn't want to die and end up in hell.

I prayed extra hard every Sunday for God to save me. I would get on my knees, and tarry and repeat the same thing over and over. "Thank you Jesus, Thank you Jesus"; as fast as I could. Sometimes I tarried so hard I would be foaming at the mouth. I felt Gods spirit a few times, or at least I thought I did. I even spoke in tongues once or twice but I didn't feel different. I still had those sick thoughts in my head, and no matter how hard I prayed I couldn't seem to get rid of them.

Every Sunday I'd stand to my feet, and give my testimony. The Pastor would say "tell God what you want him to do for you," and every time it was my turn, I'd ask God for the same thing; "Please heal Mama from her stroke."

I prayed, and asked God to heal mama, and two years later my prayers were answered! Mama was finally getting released from the rehabilitation center for good. The doctors said it was nothing short of a miracle that Mama, and her unborn baby survived a massive stroke. The rehabilitation had worked wonders, or at least that's what daddy believed. I knew it was all God's doing. He heard my prayers, maybe he got tired of me saying the same old thing over and over.

The day finally arrived when Mama came home. We hadn't seen her much in the past two years, and I was afraid that she would still look the same as I remembered the very first time I'd seen her after she had the stroke.

Daddy pushed her through the front door in her wheelchair, and by that time her hair had somewhat grown back. She slurred when she talked, but we could understand her just fine.

My sisters, and I would massage mama's arm and leg every day, and we took turns looking after our baby brother when Daddy was at work. We grew up fast after Mamas' stroke, because we had no choice.

While Mama was in the hospital, my grandmother Lee taught me how to cook. I would spend hours in the kitchen helping her make dinner. By the time mama came home I knew how to season and fry chicken, and make rice and gravy. I even learned how to make hot water cornbread from scratch, and I was only nine.

My sisters and I would cook dinner whenever Daddy had to work, or if he was he was too tired. Mama would sit in her wheelchair, and instruct us on what to do, but for the most part I knew how to prepare a decent meal.

Things were getting back to normal in our household, and I wanted to tell Mama everything that happened to me when she was gone. My sister Tina told me not to say anything because Mama was still too sick, and all it would do was worry her, so I never said a word.

A few months after Mama came home her friends finally came to visit. None of them had bothered to come see her in the hospital or see us when she was gone.

Mama couldn't get rid of them before she got sick, and it made me angry to see those fake people coming over our house laughing and drinking; pretending to care about us, and Mama.

They even had the nerve to take mama to a night club in her wheel chair, but when they realized Mama couldn't party with them like she did before, they gradually stopped coming to visit.

My sisters, and I told Mama all about the church across the street, and how nice the people were. We told her that if she didn't get saved; she was going to burn in hell with all the sinners. At first she thought we were brain washed, but after a few months of begging; Mama finally decided to go to church with us.

I told her that if she asked God; he'd heal her arm and leg. My sisters, and I helped her get dressed; put on her wig, and we pushed her across the street in her wheel chair. From that day on, Mama went to church every Sunday.

I'll never forget the Sunday my mother got saved. It was a warm summer day in June 1972. The church had a revival and the visiting preacher did the usual alter call. He said "if anyone wants to accept Jesus Christ as their personal savior; come to the altar". Mama rose to her feet; by then she was out of the wheel chair, and was using a cane. The doctors said she'd never walk again, but God proved them wrong again.

Mama slowly walked to the altar; dragging her left leg; her arm curled up next to her side. She fell to the floor; tears flowing like rivers of water. She cried out to God in a voice so pitiful it made everyone in the church cry. She shouted! "God I'm not leaving until you save me!"

Mama cried; prayed, and screamed for God to save her repeatedly. Soon all the other church members got down on their knees, and started praying with her. We sat there for hours waiting for Mama to get saved; then one of the ladies finally walked my sister's and me home.

The little church kept its doors opened all night while Mama prayed, and when she came home the next morning; she wasn't the same.

She had a glow on her face, and her eyes glistened like diamonds. Her smile, and tone of voice was different too. She seemed happy, and at peace. Mama never drank liquor, or smoked another cigarette again, and she stopped cursing to. That's when I knew Mama was saved.

God, and the little church on the corner was all she needed.

I thought mama was amazing, because she never gave up, she committed her life to God, and never looked back.

Daddy was a different story altogether. He wasn't much of a church going man, he thought most preachers were glorified pimps, and self-righteous hypocrites.

Every now and then he'd go to church just to please Mama. I knew Daddy believed in God, he just felt like some preachers put on a show; driving around in their big shiny Cadillac's, wearing their designer suits; while some of the members didn't even have a car, or decent clothes.

Our church was different. Nobody had much; including the pastor, and his wife. What little they did have; they always shared with the church members. We were like a family.

We had a small choir, that consisted of about five or six people. Mama was the lead singer. She had the voice of an angel, and every time she'd sing, "Precious Lord" everyone in the church was brought to tears.

Mama would lend a hand to everyone. It didn't matter who they were, or how they looked; she always tried to help. Sometimes the prostitutes would come to our house, and she'd pray for them, and fix them a hot meal.

I'd get angry because I thought she was giving all of our food away. We didn't have much, but Mama didn't care. She made everybody feel important, and loved, and they respected her. Somehow we never ran out of food, or went to bed hungry; no matter how much Mama gave away.

Mama had the spirit of God all over her, and you could see it in her eyes, and hear it in her voice. She was kind, and loving, and she always put God first. Mama wouldn't make a decision without praying and waiting for an answer from God.

Once she even let a prostitute name Brenda, and her baby stay with us. We didn't have much room, but Mama couldn't stand the thought of the women being out of the streets with a baby, so she welcomed her in our home with open arms. Brenda told Mama she wanted to get out of that life, and started going to church with us.

One day Brenda's pimp Silky found out where she was, and came to our house to get her. Mama wasn't afraid of anything. The minute he started yelling, and making threats; Mama started praying and pleading the blood of Jesus; rebuking the devil out of him, and eventually he gave up, and never came back.

Brenda lived with us for a few months, she told me about her life, and how she ran away from home when she was just fifteen years old, because her mother was a drug addict, and would sell her to different men for drugs.

Brenda said she stayed in abandoned buildings, and ate food from the garbage; until the day she met Silky, and he promised her a better life. She said everything was good at first. She had a place to stay, clothes to wear, and food to eat.

When she got pregnant, and refused to sell her body; Silky threatened to kill the baby, so she continue to prostitute until the baby she went into labor.

I felt sorry for Brenda. She had a rough life, and no one who really loved her. I admired her strength, and honesty, and the fact that she treated me like I was a grown-up. She told me the truth about the cold cruel world, and I was afraid to grow up.

One day I came home from school, and she was gone. I immediately asked mama where she was, and all she said was "Brenda had to leave".

I tried to pry more information out of mama, but she sent me on my way. I wasn't satisfied with the answer, but I dare disobey mama, because I didn't want the wrath of God coming down on me.

I was heartbroken that Brenda didn't bother to say goodbye, but I just prayed I would never see her standing on the corner selling her body for Silky again.

Every Saturday our Church would sell barbeque dinners to raise money for the building fund. I would volunteer to help, because Mother Stevens would always give me snacks, and occasionally I'd get a rib, or piece of chicken out of it too.

As bad as our neighborhood was; the people respected the little church, and even the pimps, and prostitutes would stop by to buy a barbeque dinner.

Our church welcomed anyone. Sometimes in the winter some of

the prostitutes would come to church on Friday nights to get out of the cold, and they were treated with the same respect as everyone else.

Elder Stevens was in his early sixties, and wore a hearing aid. Half the time I could barely understand a word he was saying, and every so often Mother Stevens would have to translate the sermon for him.

They had two children, Penny, and Daniel. Daniel played the organ, and was very good. Mother Stevens play the piano. I don't think she had any formal training, because every note she played sounded the same. We'd sing the songs right along with her as if we didn't notice.

I wanted to be like my Mama, so I asked to sing the lead in the junior choir. My sister Tina could sing, and she led all the songs. I didn't have much of a voice, but Mother Stevens was so kind, and didn't want to hurt my feelings, so she let me lead a song anyway.

There I was standing in front of the congregation singing "Oh Happy Day". My voice was cracking, and I couldn't hold a note. Mother Stevens was banging on the piano so loud; I could barely hear myself singing.

I'm sure she was trying to drown me out, so no one else could hear how bad it was. When I finished everyone clapped. I went back to my seat feeling like I'd conquered the world. Mama sat on the front row looking at me with a big smile on her face, and that meant everything to me.

Every time I saw Mama get the Holy Ghost; I'd get it too. I would jump up, and down with my eyes half closed; peeking around to see if anyone was looking. Then I'd fall on the floor kicking, and screaming. Most of the time I was faking, and would hurt myself. I wouldn't say anything because I didn't want Mama to know; although I think she knew, and just never said anything.

The day I got baptized was one of the best days of my life. I put on this white robe, and stepped into the freezing cold water. Elder Stevens was waiting inside wearing rubber overalls like a fisherman. My lips were trembling, and my body was shaking.

Pastor Stevens anointed my head with holy oil; prayed for me, covered my nose and mouth; then dunked me in the water. When I came out; I felt different. I just knew my life was about to change and everything would be alright.

The church was the one place in the world that I felt safe, and loved. When I was ten years old I joined an after school bible program. I memorized all the books of the bible from Genesis to revelations, and could quote scriptures from memory.

I competed in several bible contest, and won numerous trophies, and medals. I took great pride in that accomplishment, because I made mama, and the church proud of me.

We shared good times, and bad. We had church picnics, and barbeques; funerals, and weddings. The best thing we shared was love. They loved us, and we loved them.

Elder Stevens passed away from heart failure, and the little church shut its doors for good. I don't know how they managed to stay open as long as they did. The church didn't make much money with the few members in the congregation. I'm sure elder, and Mother Stevens must have been paying most of the overhead from their own pocket just to keep the doors open.

I was heartbroken just knowing the one place I found comfort, and solitude was now gone. I didn't want to go to another church, because I didn't trust very many people. I didn't want to get close to anyone else fearing they would die.

I'd witnessed many miracles in that tiny little church. In my heart; I believed Elder, and Mother Stevens helped save mama's life the day they knocked on our door inviting us to church.

Mother Stevens died a few years after her husband. They said it was from a heart attack, but I think she died from a broken heart.

I cried for days just knowing I would never see her smile or hear her lovely voice again. I missed her playing that same ole tune over, and over on that beat up piano. I missed singing "Jesus is the light of the world" and most of all I miss those stale macaroon cookies, and punch every Sunday morning.

Some of my fondest memories were in that little church on the corner; with its small make shift alter, and it eight wooden benches. Everything I'd ever known about God was taught to me in that church, and although I went astray I never forgot my roots.

Everything in my life began to change, and I realized nothing would ever be the same again.

Chapter Four

Behind Closed Doors

My childhood was beginning to get better. I was in the sixth grade now, and although I still had nightmares about Eula every now and then, they didn't consume my dreams as much as they had in the past.

I gave up trying to understand why she did those things to me, and no one else. I felt there had to be something wrong with me, because she only chose me too physically, and sexually abuse.

I prayed, and asked God to help me forget about all the bad things she'd done to me, but the memories never disappeared. So I kept them hidden deep below the surface, and pretended everything was fine. It was like I had split personalities, one part of me was good, and the other part was evil. One minute I'd be talking and laughing and the next minute I'd be cursing and fighting.

Once I got into a fight with a boy name Patrick in my sixth grade class because he made fun of my mother. He called her a "Crip" because she was cripple. I picked up a chair and tried to hit him with it, and my teacher intervened and sent me to the principal's office. I had an uncontrollable temper and I couldn't oppress my rage.

Sometimes I would get so embarrassed when mama came to the school, because I didn't want the kids to make fun of her. On the surface I appeared to be normal, but in the inside I was lost and confused.

I lived in a fantasy world; no one knew just how bad I felt about myself. It was better to pretend then to face reality, and I had mastered the art of pretending.

I excelled academically in school, and from kindergarten to the sixth grade I made excellent grades, but I was angry and rebellious. I got into fights all the time because I refused to let anyone bully me. I felt that I had to protect myself from everyone or they would take advantage of me.

I feared everything, yet I hid it from everyone by acting out in anger. I kept a journal, and wrote down all my thoughts and feelings daily because I couldn't tell anyone for fear they would judge me.

Sometimes I would suffer from severe chest pains, and my parents would rush me to the hospital over and over, and the doctors would examine me, and they could never find anything wrong. As I got older I realized I was having anxiety attacks because I held so much inside.

I had so much hatred, and bitterness in my heart about be poor and black. I despised all the television shows about black families living in the ghetto or housing projects; while the white shows pictured kids living in lavish homes with butlers and maids.

I lived in the ghetto, so why would I want to watch a show about poor people like me? I'd fantasize about how much better it would be if I were white.

I was so ashamed of being black that I would tell kids at school that I was adopted, and that my real parents were white, and that they were coming to get me!

I was light skinned, with dark brown eyes and long black wavy hair, I favored my mother's side of the family more than my fathers, but anyone could clearly see that by no stretch of the imagination I was white.

I'm sure the kids at school all thought I was crazy. They never said anything to my face because they knew I had a temper and didn't mind fighting if I was challenged.

It didn't take much to make me angry, and I'd fight anyone, boy or girl; big or small. Most of the time I was scared, but I refused to back down or show an ounce of fear.

I never understood why my grandmother with her long fine wavy hair flowing down her back; green eyes and white skin complained about being half white.

As far as I was concerned to me she was lucky, because being black was a curse in my eyes. Being white meant you were superior, and everyone respected and feared white people weather they were a millionaire or a bum under a bridge.

My neighborhood was predominantly black. We had one Hispanic family on our street, and they barely spoke English and never came outside.

Our street was very small. At one end was a busy main street and at the other was the harbor freeway. There were sixteen houses in total.

The majority of families on out block had both a mother, and father figure in the household. Everyone's life seemed normal on the outside, but that was far from the truth.

There were things that were going on behind closed doors, and even if we heard rumors about anyone we knew better than to repeat anything that was said.

One of my best friends was a girl name Candace, her family nicknamed her Pumpkin so that's what everyone called her.

Pumpkin was a few months older than me. She was a pretty brown skinned girl, with big light brown eyes, and deep dimples in both cheeks. She had a big smile with exquisite teeth. Pumpkin had long legs, and was tall, and skinny.

We had a lot in common. We both loved to dress up, and we both wanted to be models when we grew up. Pumpkin was much taller than me with long fingers, and luxurious nails that were at least a half inch long.

Pumpkin lived down the street with her mother, step-father and five siblings. She was the oldest, and she had one sister, and three brothers.

Their family had more money than ours; because they had two cars and a boat. Her step-father owned a small neighborhood meat market, and her mother worked too.

Pumpkin at the meat market on the weekends, and during the summer. Her step-father would let some of the neighborhood kids' work to earn extra money too. I thought he was one of the nicest grown-ups around because he always greeted me with a smile and a hug.

He seemed friendly, and kind but Pumpkin loathed him. I couldn't understand why until one weekend when I spent the night over her house. It was Pumpkins' 11th birthday and she invited me, and my sister Mia to a small pajama party.

There were just five girls at the sleep over. Mia and I, Pumpkin's sister Gina; who we nicknamed "Breath" because she had bad halitosis, and her older cousin Tanya. She was supposed to be supervising the party because Pumpkins' mother worked nights. All she did was stay in the back room and talk on the phone to her boyfriend.

The night started out fine, we played board games, told some ghost stories, and painted our nails. The night was going good until Pumpkin went into the kitchen to get us something to drink.

I saw her step-father go into the kitchen with a plate in his hand; I got up to ask if I could have something to eat, and as I walked to the narrow opening of the kitchen; I witnessed her step-father put the plate on the counter; and before I could say anything; I saw him rub his hand across her back; down to her butt, and between her legs!

I couldn't believe what I was seeing. I hurried back to the living room, and sat down. A few minutes later Pumpkin ran out of the kitchen; spilling our drinks all over her. She looked afraid, but I didn't say anything, and neither did she.

I just pretended nothing happened. That night I wanted to go home; but I was afraid to tell her for fear I'd hurt her feelings. So I laid on the floor next to her on top of some old musty blankets that smelled like feet and fart, and tried to go to sleep.

It was hard to close my eyes, but I drifted off to sleep, and what happened next shocked me. I was awakened in the middle of the night by the touch of someone's hand caressing my thigh.

I could feel my heart pounding through my night shirt, but I was too scared to open my eyes for fear of what was going to happen next, so I pretended to be sleep.

The fondling went on for a while. I could feel a hand underneath my shirt rubbing my flat chest, and gently pulling my nipples, and then the hand moved down, and found its way into my pajama bottoms, and gently caressed my vagina.

All I could think about was Eula, and a sickening feeling came over me; fear raced through my body as I began to tremble. Then suddenly the fondling stopped. I kept my eyes shut as tight as I could until the person turned over, and went to sleep. It was Pumpkin!

I never went back to sleep that night, and as soon as the sun came up I got dressed, woke up my sister Mia, and we walked home without saying a word. I didn't say anything to anyone.

I began to believe that it was my fault that this happened again, although I never told Pumpkin what happened to me, I started to believe that I did something to make her think it was okay.

I avoided Pumpkin for a few weeks; then one day while playing in the backyard alone she showed up. She asked me if I was mad at her, and she said she was sorry, and before I knew it we were kissing passionately.

She told me that her step-father had been molesting her for years, and that she was afraid to tell her mother because he had threatened her. I told her what Eula did to me, and we found comfort in each other, because at least we weren't doing anything to hurt each other.

I knew in the eyes of God, and the church that what I was doing was wrong. For some reason no matter how hard I prayed and asked God to take those feelings away from me they didn't stop.

Pumpkin understood how I felt inside, because she was enduring the same sexual abuse. My sisters didn't know how I felt and it seemed that they'd forgotten all about what happened to me as soon as we got home.

I was damaged, my innocence had been seized and I felt lost inside myself. I prayed and asked God to forgive me every time I did it, but I loved Pumpkin and she loved me, and in our own dysfunctional way we made each other feel good about ourselves. The sexual relationship between Pumpkin, and I lasted over two years, and it was our little secret.

As time passed I think my mother begin to suspect something, because she stopped letting us have pajama parties, and soon Pumpkin, and I went our separate ways.

Pumpkin grew up to become a beautiful women. She married right after high school, because she was so desperate to get away from her stepfather.

From the outside looking in, she seemed to have the perfect life, and I envied her. Things aren't always the way they appear on the surface, and although Pumpkin had a good job, a nice car, and a big house she didn't seem happy. She still wore that fake smile that I was familiar with when we were kids.

I heard through the neighborhood grapevine that Pumpkin's husband left her for another woman, and took their son. The failure of her marriage, and losing her son devastated her so badly that she turned to drugs, and became addicted to heroin and cocaine. She died at the ripe ole age of thirty-two from AIDS.

Pumpkin was just was just one of many girls I had sexual encounters with growing up, because I was so confused about my sexuality. The church taught me one thing, but life's experiences taught me another.

Our neighborhood had its share of crazy, dysfunctional people, and every household held their own secrets. One of my closest friends growing up was a boy name Teddy.

Teddy was tall with caramel skin, hazel eyes, and an infectious smile. He was very handsome, and could pass for a male model. My sisters and I nicknamed him "Tink" short for Tinkerbelle the fairy because he was gay.

His mother, step-father and two younger brothers moved to our neighborhood when he was ten. I knew Tink was different the moment I laid eyes on him. He always wanted to play with me, and my sisters, and he didn't have any interest in girls or sports at all. I was more of a tom-boy then Tink was.

Every time we played kick ball he'd stand on the curb and cheer like a girl. Which was a sheer indication that he was gay. Not to mention the fact that he talked and walked like a girl, and always wanted to squeeze in my clothes and prance around our bedroom like he was a runway model.

He was the only boy allowed in our bedroom. I guess Mama knew he wasn't a threat. Teddy shared his innermost secrets with me, and my sisters.

He told us that his mother would dress him up in girl clothes when he was little, and take pictures of him because she wanted a daughter so badly. I thought that was pretty strange behavior and that maybe she was the reason he was gay.

Tink made us promise not to tell anybody on the block that he was gay. I was good at keeping secrets, because I had so many of my own, so I made him a promise that I'd never tell.

Tink was the only person I told I liked girls, because I knew I could trust him not to tell anyone. I didn't consider myself a lesbian because I liked boys too, and although I'd never had a boyfriend I still wanted to know what it would be like to be with a boy sexually. Maybe I was in denial, or just too afraid to label myself a lesbian.

Everyone on our block knew Tink was a gay, but nobody ever said anything to his face, because they didn't want to hurt his feelings. Tinks' obvious feminist behavior made it easy to figure out.

The thing I loved about Tink the most was his confidence. He carried himself as though he didn't have a care the world, and he loved himself immensely. He'd spend hours in the bathroom prepping himself before coming outside just to sit on the steps to talk.

He dressed as though he'd just stepped out of G.Q magazine, and considering the fact that practically everything he wore was hot as fish grease, Tink boasted, and bragged as if he'd paid for it.

Once he was being bullied at school about being gay. I could see that it was taking a toll on him, so I agreed to pretend to be his girlfriend for a school dance.

Tink was a wonderful dancer, and had danced on soul train a few times, but he'd never slow danced with a girl or even gotten more than a few feet of any female except my sisters, and me. So we decided we were going to teach him how to bump and grind.

I pressed my body against his, and pulled his arms around my waist, I could feel that this made him uncomfortable by the way he kept trying to pull away. I held him tight, and rested my head on his broad shoulders.

We rocked back, and forth slowly, and I put my leg between his to show him how to grind on a woman, and suddenly Tink pushed me so hard I fell, and hit the floor. All we could do was laugh as he scrapped me off the linoleum.

Tink endured his share of prejudice, and abuse about his sexual preference, but he still managed to graduate high school with honors considering all the cruelty he faced.

He had a very promising career ahead of him as a fashion designer until he got hooked on crack cocaine. He dropped out of college and was living on the streets until he met the love of his life; a man name Vincent.

Vincent seemed like the best thing since sliced bread. He had a good career as a chef, and he had his own home in San Francisco. He moved Tink in, cleaned him up, and helped him get off drugs.

Everything appeared to be wonderful from the outside looking in. Two years into the relationship Tink was diagnosed with full blown AIDS that he contracted from Vincent.

Tink died six months later at the aged of twenty-five. I was heartbroken over his loss. It was as if a piece of me died with him.

No matter how much everyone tried to hide what was going on behind closed doors; it always had a way of getting out. Christine was one of the prettiest girls I'd ever seen. She looked white, but she was actually creole.

She had long wavy black hair, big beautiful brown eyes and a smile you couldn't forget. She lived down the street with her parents, and three siblings.

We didn't get to play much growing up, but when we'd see each other we'd always smile, and wave to one another. Christine was very nice and quiet, so when I heard she was pregnant at fourteen I couldn't believe it.

The gossip circulating around the neighborhood was that she was forced to get married, but Christine never told me that. Her boyfriend Fred couldn't be more than sixteen at the time. He was a nice looking; tall, skinny, dark skin boy from Long Beach.

There were rumors that it was a "Shot gun wedding" I didn't know what that meant at the time; all I knew was that nobody seemed to like Fred because he was controlling, and jealous.

I hardly saw Christine after she got married, and moved away and on the rare occasion she did come by I'd only get a glimpse of her getting out of the car walking into her parents' house with the baby wrapped in a blanket, and Fred walking behind her like a drill sergeant.

Christine always kept her head down, and never made direct eye contact with anyone. She looked so unhappy. I felt sorry for her. I'd heard the neighbors gossiping that her husband was beating her. I really felt bad for Christine because I knew what it was like to be abused, it didn't matter if it were a man or a women committing the abuse, it was still the same, and I didn't have to imagine what she was going through.

I prayed for her every time I saw her because I knew she had to afraid, and confused just like me. Christine had two kids with Fred and endured years of physical, mental and emotional abuse, and when she'd had enough of his torment; she packed her belongs, took her babies and left him, and never looked back. I was proud that she'd taken her life back, I wish I could have taken mine from Eula; but that never happened.

There was so much happening on our tiny little block that I failed to realize there was a whole world out there that existed. I thought every inner city neighborhood was like ours, and that everything that happened on our street was normal.

Our next door neighbor was a little old lady name Helen. We called her "Little Mama" because she was about 4'9 and weighed about 80 pounds.

She was an elderly woman in her sixties. The whites of her eyes were mustard yellow. She reeked of gin, and drank so much she had liquor coming out of her pores like perfume.

Little mama would always call me over to help her do something around her house. I tried my best to dodge her, but she would knock on the door, and ask mama if I could come help her and mama eagerly said yes.

Little mama had several cats and dogs, too many to count, and her house smelled of feces and urine. She would always manage to find something she needed me to do when her boyfriend Henry wasn't home.

Henry was a heavy set, black man with two teeth in his entire mouth. Henry was very nice, and every time he saw me he'd give me a quarter. He could usually be found standing on one of the corners with the other wine-o's getting drunk.

One day Little Mama, and Henry got into a fight. Which occurred at least once a week when they got drunk. I could hear them yelling from outside their house.

I was standing on the sidewalk playing hopscotch when she burst out the front door holding a leg in her hands. She threw it in the middle of the street; in hopes a car would drive by and run it over. All I could do was scream, because I thought she had cut off Henry's leg.

It wasn't until Henry hopped out the door, down the stairs and off the curb to pick up his other leg that I realized she didn't cut it leg off.

I ran in the house to tell Mama. She laughed and calmly said "Oh baby everybody knew Henry's leg was fake." I thought to myself "well nobody bothered to tell me!"

Little mama was a character. She wore a short curly wig flopped to the side of her head, and when she got drunk she'd take it off, and throw it in the front yard.

I couldn't imagine her ever being young or pretty. She looked worn out, and dirty, and she never wore shoes. She'd always called me "Rob-bee" and I despised that name. She'd always tell me how she could see through me, and that scared me, because I thought somehow she knew my secret.

Once she grabbed my cheeks, and squeezed so tight she left marks on my face, and from that point on every time I'd see her I'd run the opposite direction because I was afraid of her.

Little mama dropped dead in her house one hot summer day. She drank herself to death at the age of sixty-five. Henry moved out, and life kept going on.

The "Crips" had taken over our neighborhood, and like most gang infested communities we learned to adjust to it because there was nothing we could do.

My father was determined to keep us away from gangs. Most of the boys in my neighborhood had to join the gang because they were too afraid not to. You were either in the gang and protected or out of it, and subjected to whatever punishment they decided you deserved.

If an outsider happened to wonder into our neighborhood they would beat them up, and rob them. If they didn't have any money they'd take their clothes, and shoes.

Although they were thugs, most of them were nice. They were all searching for love, and acceptance just like me, and they found it in the streets.

Most of them came from single family homes, didn't know their father and lived in poverty. I never looked down on them because even though I had a father I was no better than them, because I still lived in the ghetto just like they did.

We had our share of ups, downs, sadness and joy; living in South Central Los Angeles, but for some reason I was never afraid until one night I was walking home alone.

The street lights had just come on, and I was trying to make it in the house before daddy came home, when a dark brown cargo van slowly pulled up next to me with a black man in his late twenties inside. I was fourteen years old at the time and I didn't think much of it because I thought our neighborhood was safe.

He rolled down the window, and I thought he was going to ask for directions, but instead he pointed a gun in my face, and told me to get in the van. He said if I screamed he was going to kill me, so I put my hands in the air as though I was under arrest. I looked him straight in the eyes to gesture that I understood his demands, and I walked slowly towards the van.

The man wore a dark beanie on his head, and a jean jacket. He had a thick mustache, and dark piercing eyes. When I reached the door I put my hand out, and slowly grabbed the handle. I opened the door, and a voice inside me said "Run!" and I took off in the opposite direction; running down the street screaming as loud as I could.

I made it to a neighbor's porch, and started beating on the front door, but no one answered. I ran from house to house and still no answer. I couldn't believe nobody was home.

I hid in some bushes as I watched the van speeding down the street burning rubber. When I got home, I was trembling all over, and from that day on I never felt safe, and I never walked outside alone again.

Chapter Five

When the School Bells Rang

It was September 1974; I was twelve years old when I fell in love with a boy named Demetrius. We were both in Mr. Lee's sixth grade class.

He was light skinned, with light brown eyes, and a big afro. He was the cutest boy in the school. Demetrius asked me to be his girlfriend, and that's when I begin to believe I was pretty.

We went together for a whole month, which is a lifetime in elementary school. Demetrius lived down the street from the school, and every day he'd walk me half way home, and we would hold hands, and smile back and forth at each other.

I couldn't wait for the weekend to be over just so I could see him again. Every girl in school liked him. He was the most popular boy in the sixth grade.

One Monday morning Demetrius wasn't in class, the lunch bell rang, and I ran to find his twin sister Dana to see why he didn't come to school. To my surprise she wasn't at school either.

On the way home I passed by their house; I was too afraid to knock on the door so I stood across the street staring at the house in hopes he would look out the window, but he never did, so I went home.

The next morning when I arrived at school Demetrius still wasn't there. Our principal called all the six grade students, and teachers into the auditorium, and made an announcement that would devastate me forever.

He stood on the stage in his black suit; white shirt, and strip tie. He had a sad look on his face, then he cleared his throat as though something was stuck in it. In a somber voice he announced that Demetrius had died from an asthma attack."

My chest started to hurt, and suddenly I found it difficult to breath.

I began to scream, and cry uncontrollably. I had never known anyone who had died before. I jumped to my feet, and ran out the door.

Mr. Lee ran after me, but this time it was because I'd did something wrong in class. He knew Demetrius, and I were an item. He sat me down on a bench by the hand ball court, and hugged me, and told me everything was going to be alright.

I really loved Mr. Lee, because he cared about how I felt, and he was the only teacher I could talk to. He would always listened to my side of the story before assuming I was wrong, and he'd tell me the raw truth in a nice, caring way.

I thought Demetrius was too young to die, after all he was just twelve years old. What did Demetrius do? Why did he have to die? These questions were racing through my mind. I couldn't understand why God let this happen.

My heart was broken in a thousand pieces. The principle called mama, and she came and got me. As we walked home that day, I stopped and stared at Demetrius's tiny little house. The curtains were closed, and it looked empty, and dark.

I went home, and sat in the back yard, and cried until my eyes were swollen shut. I looked up to the sky through the tiny slits in my eyes, and asked God to please take care of Demetrius for me.

The next week my entire class attended his funeral. There he was lying motionless in his tiny little casket. He wore a brown suite, white shirt, and a beige tie. He looked as though he was asleep.

I put my hand on his handsome face, it felt cold, and hard. I stood there in disbelief, because I'd never seen anyone dead before. I could hear his mother sobbing as she sat on the front row of the church across from his lifeless body. His twin sister sat slumped down next to her with her face in her hands. It was one of the saddest days of my life.

Elementary school would never be the same. I would never be the same. I was angry at God for letting Demetrius die. I feared death, and the thought of someone being placed in a coffin and dropped in the ground with dirt on top of them made me afraid.

I always thought to myself "what if they weren't really dead and they awakened from their deep sleep, and called out for help and nobody hears them?"

Dying became one of my biggest fears. At night I would lay in bed while my sisters slept, and I'd see a tall man in a black hat and coat come into our room. I couldn't see his face, but I could hear him breath. He would stand there glaring at me. I could feel my heart racing, and I would close my eyes as tight as I could and pray that he would leave. He never did anything to me, but I felt a sense of fear whenever he came around.

My sister's said they saw him too. When I told Mama, she said that God sends angels in all forms, and that it was probably my guardian angel protecting me.

I wondered where my guardian angel was when Eula was doing all those bad things to me. Why didn't he protect me then?

The time had come for me to graduate from the sixth grade. I was chosen to write a speech, and read it at my graduation ceremony.

Mr. Lee always had told me how intelligent I was, so he chose me to speak on behalf of our class. It took weeks for me to prepare my speech. I was excited that I was one of four students selected to speak.

I wrote about the importance of having an education, and when it was my turn, I held my head up high; pranced up to the stage with my long floral dress, and my hair in Shirley temple curls. I felt just like a movie star. All eyes were on me. I started to get butterflies in my stomach, and my hands began to shake.

I had memorized every word, and as I began to recite it, I could see the flashes from Daddy's camera as he stood in front of the audience taking pictures. He looked so proud.

When I finished, the crowd began to clap, and they gave me a standing ovation. I walked off the stage with so much pride, and determination. I just knew that I was going to be someone great one day.

Daddy and mama hugged me, and told me I did a great job, and that I made them very proud, and that meant everything to me.

We all loaded up in the car, and went to Bob's Big Boy to celebrate. That was one of the best days of my young life. I kept that speech in my journal, and from time to time I would read it just to remind me of that proud moment in my life.

It was June 1975 when I was promoted to the seventh grade. My parents were determined not to let us become a product of our environment, so they decided to have us desegregated.

We were bussed to a school two hours away from home, because daddy wanted us to get the same education as the white kids.

I didn't want to go on some long bus ride hours away from home to a strange school with people different from me. I wanted to stay in the place I was familiar with, even though there was some bad elements, and not many positive role models.

I became accustom to that atmosphere. I still felt a sense of security in that environment as crazy as it may seem. I guess it all stems from what happened to me when I went to visit my Aunt several years ago.

I feared the unknown. After watching "ROOTS", and listening to all the stories, my grandmother told me about the Ku Klux Klan; I despised white people, and feared them, because I knew what they were capable of doing to us. They had money and power, and could buy their way out of anything while we were nobody and had nothing.

It was always hard for me to sleep the night before the first day of school. I prepared for it as if I was going to a corporate job. I would lay my school clothes out on the chair with my new shoes placed neatly beside them. I'd tie a scarf around my head, and hang it off the side of the bed to make sure I didn't mess up my curls. That was the only day other then picture day that momma would let me wear my hair down.

I was usually excited about the first day of school, but this time wasn't like the usual night before school jitters; I felt a sense of apprehension and anxiety.

My sister Tina and I were in bed by seven o' clock, because we had to get up at five-thirty to get ready for school. We were one of two other families on our street that was forced to attend the white school. All the other kids got to attend the black junior high school that was walking distance from where we lived.

My sister Tina, and I walked to the bus stop in the dark. When we reached our destination there were kids standing in groups laughing, and cracking jokes.

When the school bus pulled up to the curb, we all formed a single line, and started to board the bus. My sister Tina had struggled with her weight ever since I could remember; and I didn't know why she was fat because she ate the same things we did. I knew it bothered her even though she never said anything. The unhappy look in her eyes said it all.

When it was time for us to go school shopping; Mama would always have to go to a different store to find her clothes. Sometimes Tina would even try to starve herself to lose weight; but nothing she did seemed to work.

As she stepped on the school bus the kids started making pig noises and rocking the bus as if there was an earthquake. I could see that she was upset and embarrassed. I knew she wouldn't say anything, so I began cursing them out. The bus driver intervened and told everyone to shut up. Tina and I made our way to our seats; he put the bus in gear, and we were on our way.

After a ride that seemed to take forever. We finally exited the freeway headed to our new school in the valley.

My stomach was in knots, and my hands were sweating. The neighborhoods were beautiful with tree lined streets; big beautiful houses and fancy cars. It was nothing like our neighborhood. I didn't see one drunk or drug addict.

There were no liquor stores or motels anywhere. There were no run-down dope houses or prostitutes on the corner. It was clean and neat; a place I had always fantasized about but never thought I'd see.

Suddenly our bus pulled up in front of the school, and what happened next was far from what I could ever envisioned. We were greeted with rocks, and bottles being thrown at the bus.

They spray painted the front of the school in big bold black spray paint; "Boating not Bussing, Niggas' go back to Africa!"

Our bus driver started the engine, and took off. I was so afraid I started to cry. Some of the kids on the bus got hit with the rocks and pieces of broken bottles as they shattered against the open windows on the bus.

The bus driver circled around until he found a local park, and we sat there for hours until the police arrived, and escorted us back to the school.

When we returned all the students were gone. I could see some of them staring at us from the classroom windows. The principal ushered us off the bus like a herd of cattle and placed us in the auditorium until they could figure out what to do next.

When I got home I just knew mama and daddy wouldn't make us go back, but they said we had to fight for what we believed in like Martin Luther King. I didn't want to fight, because I didn't believe we belonged there in the first place, but they kept sending us back.

They finally got us into our class rooms about two week later, and that's when all the rioting began. I never understood why every race was against the blacks. I thought the Mexicans should have been on our side since they were minorities too, but they went along with the whites just like every other race.

For weeks we fought. There were police on campus, and helicopters flying overhead. The news media was reporting about the riots too. I just didn't know what we were fighting about; until one day I came face to face with racism.

It was a Friday afternoon, and I was running late for my sixth period class. I ran into the girls' bathroom to avoid peeing on myself. While I was in the stall two white girls came in.

When I opened the door they just stared at me, and begin whispering. I walked to the sink to wash my hands as they headed out the bathroom. Before the door closed I heard them say "Why don't those Nigga's go back where they came from?"

Before I knew what hit me; I ran out of the bathroom, and pushed one of the girls down the stairs. The other girl ran the opposite direction as I stood at the top of the stairs too paralyzed to move.

I was suspended from school for a week, the white girl fractured her ankle, and sustained minor bruises. It was the price I had to pay to gain respect. All I could think of was "I bet she won't call nobody else a Nigga".

I was more fearful of what was going to happen to me when I got home then I was about getting suspended from school. Although mama only had one good arm; she packed a punch like Muhammad Ali.

That day I walked home from the bus stop as slow as I could; in fear of what mama was going to do to me. I got the beating of my life that day, but in the end it was worth it.

The fighting stopped shortly after that, and eventually everything started to change when a few of the black boys made the football team. They started winning games then suddenly they were acknowledged.

As time passed I'd see the white cheerleaders walking around with the black football players; giggling and batting their fake eyelashes.

The sad thing was that the black boys started treating us like we were gum under their shoes. It made me angry to see them acting like they were too good for us now that they were accepted into the white world.

When they got on the school bus headed back to the ghetto, I made of point of reminding them where they came from. I always had a smart mouth, and a sharp tongue, so when I asked them if they were going to bring their white girlfriends to the ghetto; they just sit there looking stupid; staring out the window, without saying a word.

My best friend in Junior high was a girl name Sandra. She was a light skinned, Carmel colored girl with light brown eyes; long hair and dimples. She was very pretty and everyone said we looked alike.

We would call each other every night to plan what we were going to wear to school. I was a few months older than her, and since Sandra didn't have any sisters' I became her big sister, and we did everything together. Sandra looked up to me, and that made me feel important.

Sandra's family did all kinds of fun, and adventurous things; like fishing and camping. They'd always take me along to keep her company. My family didn't do things like that because my mother was handicap, and it was difficult for her to walk; besides Daddy worked a lot and didn't have time to do that kind of stuff anyway.

It was fun when Sandra's family would take me places that I'd never been. They treated me just like I was family. I even called her mother mom.

We were inseparable until Sandra's family moved to a new city and she had to change schools. I was heartbroken when my best friend left me, and even though I had three sisters; I felt alone, because we had nothing whatsoever in common.

My older sister Tina was in theater and chorus. When she wasn't on the stage or singing, she was reading romance novels, and that seemed boring to me. My two younger sisters loved animals and spent most of their time rescuing stray dogs off the street and bringing them home.

I couldn't stand the thought of a dog or cat licking or jumping on me. Sandra and I liked the same things. We loved to dress up, wear make-up and style our hair. I cried for weeks after she left. I didn't want another best friend after that, so I spent the first few months of eighth grade alone.

As time passed things at school got better, we all learned to adapt, and get along. I even had a few white friends, and to be honest they treated me better than most the black girls did. I always seemed to have a problem with the dark skinned black girls. For some unknown reason they just didn't like me.

I was intelligent, outspoken and funny. People always told me I was pretty, but I never thought so. I just thought I was average looking.

I had long black wavy hair, light skin and dark brown eyes. I was petite with an eighteen inch waist, small breasts and curvy hips.

For some reason the dark skinned girls always tried to pick fights with me. Although I was frightened deep down inside, I put on an act. I remembered what Mama told me, "If somebody hits you; you better pick up something and knock their brains out" so I took that literally, and I would never show fear.

I hid my terror from everyone because I was good at it. I guess the things I'd experienced growing up in South Central Los Angeles had made that easy for me to do.

I wanted people to like me; so I tried to fit in even if it meant doing things I really didn't want to do. Like smoking cigarettes, marijuana and drinking alcohol. I didn't really like it, but I did it just to look cool.

I really wanted to be a cheerleader; one of the popular girls, but my parents couldn't afford it. So I pretended it was ridiculous and lame in front of the "Mean Girls" who were my "so called friends".

I wanted to take drama classes, and perform in school plays, but the "Mean Girls" said that was stupid too. So I went along with them and didn't do that either. I found myself in the principal's office every week for something bad I'd done. I thought I was a leader, but in reality I was a follower.

I did everything I didn't want to do just to please someone else; and just when I thought they liked me, they all turned on me and try to jump me.

They went as far as trying to cut my hair in the girl's bathroom one day. Luckily I had a letter opener in my pocket that I had stolen out of the teacher's desk. I started slashing at them like a cornered animal and they ran. It seemed no matter how hard I tried to make people like me; nothing I did was sufficient.

I was suspended from school countless times, because I thought I had something to prove. If I thought the teacher was talking down to me; I had no problem throwing a chair across the room, cursing them out and walking out of class.

I always felt insignificant and inadequate; like something was wrong with me. I kept that hidden behind phony smiles and laughter. I spent hours in the bathroom mirror at home talking to myself as if I was holding a conversation with somebody else.

I felt like nobody would accept me for who I really was; so I portrayed myself as someone confident and self-assured. The personality I assumed was a bad girl; but in reality I had a heart of gold, and would give the shirt off my back to anyone who needed it.

I chose wrong over right because it was easier; and I settled for whatever anyone was willing to give because I wanted to be recognized and loved.

Chapter Six

All Smoke and Mirrors

It was March 1976; I had just turned fourteen, and strangely enough I was still playing with dolls. My Barbie collection meant the world to me. All the girls I knew were interested in boys and sex, but not me; I had a goal. I was going to be a runway model and fashion designer. My parents couldn't afford modeling school, so they found a way to come up with the money to get a photographer to take pictures of me for a portfolio. His name was Steve Jacobs; I'd found him in the Los Angeles Times new paper.

Steve claimed he'd made a lot of models famous, and that he could help me too. He said I was a stunning natural beauty, and that boosted my self-esteem. I begin to take great pride in my appearance from that day on.

I reminisced back when I was little. I would put on my good Sunday dresses; stand outside, and prance around the front yard as if I was on a runway.

Although my clothes were mostly brought on clearance or thrift store finds, I would alter them to make them look brand new.

I grew to love my body, and was proud of my figure. I made a point of always wearing a short top to show off my flat stomach and tiny 18 inch waist; not an inch of body fat. I loved to swim; play tennis, and exercise. I even ran track so I could be in tip top shape.

I stood 5'5 ninety-eight pounds at fourteen, and Steve said the camera loved me. I think he said that to all the girls to build their confidence, and it worked for me. He told me I was going to be a super model, and that my face would be plastered on billboards across the country, and everybody would know my name.

It was a hot Saturday afternoon when Mr. Jacobs called. He told me he had good news, and asked if my parents were home. When

I told him they weren't home, he said he needed me to come to his office in Hollywood as soon as possible.

I was too afraid to catch the bus that far by myself, so I asked my sister Mia and cousin La'shawn to go with me. I made them promise not to tell anybody, because I thought this was going to be my big break, and I wanted it to be a surprise.

When we arrived at his office, I made them wait outside while I went in to find out the good news. I was shocked that his office wasn't in a big fancy building like all the others on Sunset Blvd.

It was an old run-down building on top of a store front. I went in with the highest expectations of becoming a model. My heart was beating so fast I could hardly breathe.

When I reached the third floor, I got off the elevator, and walked toward what I thought was going to be this big elaborate photography studio.

I was disappointed to see this dirty beige colored door that only said Suite D on the front of it. The name of his Photography studio was nowhere to be found.

At first I thought I was in the wrong building; after all, he claimed to have worked with a lot of famous models, but I couldn't image any supermodels like Twiggy, Beverly Johnson or Cheryl Tiegs ever gracing a place like this.

I knew everyone had to start somewhere. I was too naïve, and dumb to be scared, and too stupid to turn around and leave. So I knocked on the door in anticipation of what good news he had for me.

I heard a man's voice echo from the other side of the door to come in. I slowly turned the knob,and strolled inside. He didn't even have a secretary or a front office, it was just a tiny little room with a small window; a desk, two chairs and a small dirty couch that looked as though it had seen better days.

There were no pictures on the walls; which I thought was strange since he claimed he was a famous photographer to the stars.

He smiled at me, and asked me to have a seat. I was so excited I couldn't restrain myself; so I quickly asked him what the good news was. He told me to call him Steve, but I was raised not to address any grown-up by their first name, so I called him Mr. Jacobs.

He was a scraggly looking white man, with long dirty blonde hair, a mustache and beard. He was tall, and thin and looked like a hippy. He wasn't much to look at, but he seemed harmless and from the pictures he'd shown me of all the other models he had made famous he was a good photographer.

Mr. Jacobs looked at me with a devious kind of smirk on his face and then he reached in his desk and pulled out a black leather case. He opened the book, and there I was in black and white!

He showed me each of my photographs and I was amazed to see just how beautiful I was. I sat there speechless for a moment then I asked him what should I do next? I didn't have an agent or know the first thing to do to get a modeling job.

Mr. Jacobs clasped both hands together, and rested his chin on them. Then in a deep voice he said, "I can do big things for you that can open doors for your modeling career." My eyes grew wide as I sat upright in my chair. He said he would make me famous, but that I had to do something for him.

I begin to get nervous when he started licking his lips, and smiling at me like a hungry wolf. He went on to say that he liked women with small breast, and big hips; in the back of my mind I said to myself, "I'm not a woman" I'm only fourteen.

Steve was an old man; at least thirty years old if not older. He said all I had to do was give him oral sex, and let him have oral sex with me, and he could make me a star.

I could feel the tears began to well up in the corners of my eyes. I wanted to grab my pictures and run, but for some reason my feet wouldn't move. I really aspired to be a model; but at what cost? I asked myself how far I was willing to go to become a star.

Mr. Jacobs convinced me this was the only way. He said it would cost thousands of dollars to launch a modeling career, and he knew my parents couldn't afford it. They could barely afford the three hundred dollars he charged for the pictures.

I knew I couldn't burden them for more money, and I just couldn't let this opportunity pass me by. I started to try to rationalize the situation, after all Eula had done that to me when I was seven, and

Pumpkin and I had done it several times, so how bad could it be?

My heart was pounding harder than it was when I first arrived. Before I knew it, I was undressed from the waist down; lying on his desk with my legs spread wide open, and my eyes shut tight.

I wanted him to hurry up, and get it over with, so I could go home, and forget this ever happened. He submerged his hairy face between my legs, and began to lick, and suck on my clit.

He stuck his tongue inside of my vagina, and anus. I'd never experienced anything like that before. It felt nasty, and I wanted him to stop. He plunged his finger in my butt while he ate me out, and the pain was unbearable. I endured this for fifteen or twenty minutes.

When it was my turn to do him, he pulled this little pink, limp hairy thing out of his pants, it looked like a hairy worm; I bent down on my knees, and he grabbed my hand to make me touch it, suddenly I begin to vomit all over him.

He pushed me away, and jumped to his feet. He gave me some napkins so I could clean up. He told me to put on my clothes, and made me swear I wouldn't say anything to anyone.

He promised that he would still make me a superstar. When I got outside, Mia and La'Shawn were anxiously waiting by the entrance. They asked me how it went, so I showed them the pictures without saying a word, and we walked to the bus stop to catch the bus home.

A few weeks passed, and I tried to erase what I'd done with Mr. Jacobs. I convinced myself that this was a sacrifice I had to make to become famous. I thought it was only a matter of time before Mr. Jacobs would call with good news.

I arrived home from school to find a note on the refrigerator that said "Whoever gets home first, clean up the kitchen".

Well that was my unlucky day. I took off my school clothes, and went into the kitchen to wash the dishes. My mother had some red beans in a crock pot on the kitchen counter that had been cooking all day.

When I finished washing, and drying the dishes, I got down on my knees to open a drawer and the cord from the pressure cooker got tangled on the knob and in a split second it tumble over.

The glass top hit me in the head, and the scorching hot beans and water came pouring down all over me. It was so hot it cooked a hole through the powder blue and white sweater I was wearing.

I fell on the kitchen floor covered in scolding hot water and beans. I screamed for my father who was home that day for help. The burning was so intense I couldn't speak; all I could do was

scream at the top of my lungs in agonizing pain. It was a feeling I could never imagine, and one I will never forget.

As I lay there on the floor my body felt as though someone had submerged me in a hot frying pan full of grease. My hands, wrists and finger tips were burned. My stomach thighs, and vagina were all cooked. The heat was so intense it cooked all the pubic hair off my vagina. I could smell my flesh burning, and blisters starting to form over my body.

All I could think about was Elder Stevens saying how the fire in hell would be ten times hotter, and I felt like I had died and gone to hell. My father put me in the bed and went to the store to get some gauze and burn spray. He wrapped me up, and left me in the bed.

I laid there in, and out of consciousness until my mother got home, and by that time my body had gone into shock! I was rushed to hospital burn unit, and immediately submerged in an ice bath.

The doctors said if I gotten there a few minutes later; I would have died from shock. I was hospitalized with second, and third degree burns over twenty percent of my body.

I fell into a deep depression; thoughts of suicide crossed my mind often. I soon became addicted to pain pills, and even when I wasn't in pain I would lie and tell the nurse I was, just so I could get more pain medication.

The nurses would come in three times a day to change my bandages. I made a point not to look; for fear of what I was going to see. The day I was being released the nurse came in to teach me how to clean and change my bandages. I had no choice; I had to look at my body and what I saw was horrifying.

I cried so hard I could scarcely hear what the nurse was saying. She tried to console me, but it was no use. My once flawless body was destroyed; I was disfigured and my dreams of being a model were washed away by a crock pot full of beans, and there was nothing I could do about it.

The doctor said the scars were permanent, and that the only way to hide them would be to get plastic surgery; which was thousands of dollars. I knew my parents couldn't afford to pay for that, so I just accepted my fate and pretended to be ok. I tried my best to live with it; but deep inside I hated them for letting this happen to me.

All I could think of was why me? My body was the one thing I had to be proud of, and it was taken from me like everything else. I stopped believing that God loved me that day, and I didn't care what happened to me after that. There was no hope. My dream of being a famous model was over before it began.

In my mind I was hideous. I could no longer wear a bikini or look at my naked body in the mirror with pride. From that day on, I made sure to turn away from the mirror to keep from looking at myself.

The body I once adored was now the body I despised. I felt ugly inside and out; yet I never told a soul. I painted on a smile and pretended all the time, but deep inside I was bitter and angry.

I let some nasty old white man touch my body and put his mouth on me in places most couldn't even imagine, and it was all for nothing! I never told anyone what I'd done, because I was too ashamed to expose just how desperate I was to be famous.

Only God, Mr. Jacobs and I knew the scandalous things I'd done. I put that skeleton in the closet with all the rest, and I locked the door. I put on my mask and hid it from the world like everything else.

The pain of failure was unbearable for me. I had bragged to everyone that I was going to be a famous model. I had dreamed of the moment my name would be up in lights for everyone to see, but that day would never come.

To make matters worse, when my sisters got mad at me they would tie up their shirts to show their stomach, and laugh and tease me about my burns.

It hurt me so bad that I would go in the back yard and hide in the little shack with my dolls and cry. I would sit there for hours praying that God would let something bad happen to them, but it never did.

I felt cursed, as though God didn't love me anymore, and I didn't know why. I was angry at my mother for leaving the crock pot full of beans cooking on the counter, and my father for leaving me in that bed wrapped up in gauze.

Maybe if he had taken me to the doctor sooner the burns wouldn't have been so bad. I was mad at my sister's because it didn't happen to them, and I was mad at God for letting it happen to me.

The one thing I had to be proud of was taken from me in a matter of seconds, and nobody seemed to realize just how much it had affected me. Life just went on in our household; it was almost like nothing happened. Everyone moved on but me. I stood still, and let the disappointment; hurt and pain devour me.

I was dying slowly inside, and nobody had a clue. Sometimes I would fantasize about setting the house on fire, so I could kill everyone including myself. My sisters seemed to be happy and content, but I was miserable. I had no self-esteem whatsoever, no self-respect and no love for myself at all. I hated my life!

Chapter Seven

A Second Chance at Love

It was the summer of 1996 when I met a boy name James Baker. He was from Compton. His cousin Julie was my best friend on our block. They lived down the street from me and I'd spend every moment I could at their house.

James and his family always came to visit every Friday evening, and I'd make sure to be outside watering the grass just so I could get a glimpse of him when they passed by.

James reminded me of what Demetrius would look like if he had lived. He was short, light skinned, with dark brown eyes and dimples. James had a sex appeal that was out of this world.

James was sixteen when we met, and I liked him because he was cool and nonchalant. He would always make his way down to my house just to say hello to me.

He was the oldest of five brothers, and all of them were very handsome. I'd never seen brothers that were all fine.

Every time he came to visit, he'd sneak down to my house to talk to me when Daddy was at work. My father was very strict and wouldn't allow us to have boyfriends or leave the house after the street lights came on.

Daddy went as far as putting a fence around our house with a padlock on the gate to ensure we didn't get out and no one else got in. It made me feel like a prisoner.

As time passed, I saw more, and more of James and his brothers. Their family would get together all the time. Every so often I'd sneak out the house after my parents were asleep and go down to Julie's house to hang out with them.

Julie had cool parents; who let them drink, smoke cigarettes and curse. They had parties all the time, and when I learned they were from Louisiana they became my family too.

Their dad was name John, and for an older man he was extremely good looking, and down to earth. He always greeted me with a hug, and told me to call him "Pops."

Julie looked just like her mother Hattie. They were creole with light complexions, long beautiful hair, and a southern accent. They treated everyone who came to their home like family, and I was always welcomed to their house with open arms.

The summer came and my cousin Jean came to visit from Kanas. She was a beautiful dark chocolate girl; with long black hair and a lovely smile. For fifteen she was very knowledgeable about the streets.

I introduced her to James' younger brother Clarence, and they hit it off. The entire summer that Jean was there Clarence found a way to visit. I was jealous of their relationship because James didn't visit me as much, and I couldn't understand why.

His cousin Julie, and I hung out all the time after her older sister Christine got married, and moved away. She told me the reason James always came over on Friday's was because James had Leukemia, and he was in, and out of the hospital a lot. He had doctor appointments at UCLA Medical Center every Friday, so he and his family would stop by to visit before heading home.

I really liked James because he never complained about his illnesses or let it get him down. I prayed that God would heal James one day just like he healed Mama.

It was on a hot summer day in July 1976, when James finally asked me to be his girlfriend, and I gladly accepted. It seemed as though it took him forever to ask me, but I was happy he did.

Of course, I couldn't let Daddy find out, but Mama wasn't as strict so I confided in her. Sometimes she'd let James sit in the front yard, and talk to me while daddy was at work.

On a few rare occasions, Mama would even let me go down the street to Julie's house, but I had to be back before the street lights came on which wasn't very long.

James usually got there around five pm, and that's when the party began. If mama only knew I was down there drinking; smoking cigarettes, and being fast, she would never have let me go. My sister

Mia was sent to spy on me, but I converted her and before long she was doing the same thing I was doing, so I didn't have to worry about her telling on me.

I liked to drink because it helped me to relax, and I could conceal my insecurities from everyone. Sometimes I'd get so sloppy drunk I'd have to crawl home late at night; sneak in, and pass out on the floor because I couldn't make it to the bed.

It was January 1977, and my fifteenth birthday was quickly approaching. I begged Mama to let me have a birthday party, I'd never had one before, and after weeks of my begging, she finally persuaded Daddy to let me have one.

I invited a few of the kids from my neighborhood along with my cousin Jean. My sister Tina wasn't interested in attending, so Mama forced me to let my two younger sisters' Mia and Lisa come, so they could spy on me. All I really cared about was if James was coming.

When James and his brothers arrived all the girls were nervous. They were all so cool we didn't know how to act. They slipped some alcohol in the punch, and told me to turn the lights out so we could slow dance, and grind.

Every time I'd turn them off; Mia would turn them back on and threaten to tell Mama, so after of few times of lights on, lights off I gave up.

I put on a song called "Brick House" and we formed a soul train line. Now if anybody was a brick house it was my sister Mia. She had an hour glass figure; everyone would always say nice things about her shape. I must admit I was envious of her body, she had big breasts for thirteen, while I had a flat bird chest.

Mia was very anti-social when it came to boys. She claimed she didn't like them, but I knew she was insecure about the way she looked, because the boys in the neighborhood would tease her and call her ugly. They nicknamed her "Bull Dog" and went as far as carving it in wet cement on the sidewalk.

Mia wasn't ugly, she just kept a mean expression on her face which made her appear unpleasant on the eyes.

Everyone was having a good time. We were all a little tipsy from the spiked punch when Mia suddenly blurted out "Somebody Stinks!"

55

She got on her hands and knees; crawled around on the floor sniffing everyone's butt until she reached "Breath". Mia and Lisa nicknamed her 'Breath" because she had halitosis so bad it could make the hair on the back of your neck stand at attention. The crazy part was she answered to it.

Mia crawled near Breath; inhaled then she shouted "it's you!"

I was mortified! Poor Breath tried to deny it, but Mia kept pointing, and sniffing like some kind of hunting dog, and soon everybody in the room started laughing.

Finally Breath couldn't take it anymore; she ran for the front door, and that was the last we saw of her. I thought my party was ruined but James just kept slow dancing, and kissing me like no one else was there. That's the night I feel head over heels in love with him.

My first date with James was a double date with his twin sister Jessica and her boyfriend Eric. I had to beg mama and daddy for weeks to let me go. I had a twelve o'clock curfew, but that was better than nothing; I was just happy to be with James.

We drove to the Century drive-in located in Inglewood California. We saw a movie called "Saturday Night Fever" with this fine Italian boy name John Travolta.

He was one fine white boy, and if I were to cross over to the other side, it would be with him. I missed most of the movie because James, and I spent most of the time making out in the back seat.

James told me he loved me that night; and that I was beautiful, and sexy. I knew he loved me because he never pressured me to have sex with him. All the boys at school were always talking about sex, and trying to get in my panties, but James was different, he wasn't childish and immature like the boys I knew.

We spent the entire summer together, going to church picnics and to the beach. I knew that I wanted to be with him forever. I confided in Julie that James, and I were in love, and that's when she informed me that James had another girlfriend name Denise.

I was devastated, and heartbroken; I couldn't believe what I was hearing. She said they had been together at least a year before James, and I met. She said they had broken up when he met me, but that they were back together again, and she didn't want to see me get hurt.

All I could think was "how could James do this to me?" I didn't want to believe Julie. I wanted James to tell me it was a lie. I'd rather lose Julie's friendship then to lose James.

When I confronted him about it, he was honest. He told me that he loved both of us, and that he didn't want to choose. I told him I didn't want to share him with anyone else. Then he sat me down; held my hands, and looked deep into my eyes. He said "Raven, I'm not going to live very long, and I want to have all the fun I can before I die."

My heart stopped. I told him to stop talking like that, and that everything was going to be all right. At that moment, nothing else mattered. I was determined to stick it out no matter who was in the picture.

I must admit it was hard just thinking about James being with someone else, but I was willing to accept part of him rather than nothing at all.

I finally met Denise at a Christmas party at James' house. She was a dark skin girl with long black hair, dark brown eyes and full lips. She had big breasts that made my mine look like a boy's chest, and she had a huge butt that sat high on her back while my butt only had a slight hump.

I was so jealous. I wanted her to be ugly so bad, but in all honesty James had good taste. We were total opposites, but both equally beautiful in our own way. Denise, and I never physically fought over James, although sometimes I wanted to. We just stayed our distance; rolled our eyes at each other, and played along, because we both understood his situation.

Denise and I weren't friends or enemies. We just happened to love the same boy, and neither of us were willing to let him go. I found out that she had the upper hand because she had sex with James and I hadn't. I made up my mind that I was going to give myself to him so I could prove how much I loved him.

One day I caught the bus to Compton to see James. He was so sweet; he didn't rush me or make me feel like I had to have sex with him. That made what I was about to do seem right.

When I arrived at his house we went into his room. He turned on the radio, and a record by a group called Heat Wave was playing. The song was called "Always and forever".

He grabbed my hands, pulled me close, and we slow danced together. It was so sensual and romantic that I didn't want it to ever end. He started to kiss me passionately; holding me tight in his arms.

We fell on his bed; he looked in my eyes, told me he loved me with so much sincerity that I knew James was the one I wanted to lose my virginity too.

As we lay there, kissing and holding each other; he started to unbutton my blouse; then I started to panic. I didn't know what I was thinking at the time, but in order to have sex you have to take off your clothes. I thought to myself "how am I going to get out of this?" I knew if he saw me naked with that ugly scar across my stomach that he would never want to see me again.

I pretended that I was shy. I told him that I wasn't ready to take off my clothes yet. James was so considerate about my feelings that he turned off the lights, closed the curtains and told me to take off my clothes under the blanket, so I did.

James got on top of me, and started to press his small fragile body against mine. I experienced a warm tingling feeling all over my body. It was a feeling I can't describe, all I knew was it felt good.

This went on for a while, then I put my hand under the cover to feel what his penis felt like. It was soft; like a wet noodle. I didn't know what it was supposed to feel like, but I couldn't imagine how it was going to get it inside of me.

James fondled it for a few minutes; trying to make it get hard, and then after a while he gave up. I didn't say a word because I could sense his frustration as he moved from on top of me.

He laid there looking up at the ceiling in silence. He told me the medication he was taking sometimes caused him not to get an erection. I stared deep into his eyes, and told him it didn't matter to me if we had sex or not. I would wait as long as it took to be with him. I promised him that I'd never give myself to anyone else.

Deep down inside I was somewhat relieved. I really wasn't ready to have sex anyway. I just wanted to please James, and show him how much I really loved him.

I was willing to do anything to prove it. In my heart it didn't matter what we did as long as we were together. He smiled at me with that innocent sexy smile, and we laid there and held each other until it was time for me to go home. I never told any- body what happened that day, because, in my mind, we made love to each other in our hearts.

As time went on, James' health began to deteriorate. He was in the hospital more than he was home. Mama would take me up to the hospital sometimes to see him, and she would go in and pray for him. I just knew deep down in my heart that everything was going to be all right.

James had lost a lot of weight because of the Chemo- therapy and Radiation treatments. All of his beautiful hair fell out, but he was still handsome to me. I loved him no matter what, and by the spring of 1978, James was in a wheel chair, because he was too weak to walk.

I still had faith that God was going to heal James, like he did Mama. Although my prayers seemed to fall on deaf ears, I continued to pray night and day for a miracle.

I asked the church to pray for him too. I stood up every Sunday like I did when Mama was sick, and asked God to heal James from his Cancer. I was so love struck that, in my mind, I thought someday I was going to marry him, and have his children.

James graduated from Compton High School that June. I was right there by his side as they wheeled him across the stage to accept his diploma. By the end of October 1978, he was in the hospital again. The doctors had performed a bone marrow procedure on him using his sister Linda as a donor. The surgery was a success, and I knew God had worked a miracle.

A week later James died from an allergic reaction to some medication. I couldn't believe God would let something like this happen. It was November 1978 when I lost the love of my life. He was only eighteen years old.

Once again the dreams that I had for my life began to crumble. At sixteen I started to believe I was cursed. Every boy I loved seemed to die. First Demetrius; now James.

For weeks I couldn't eat or sleep; all I could do was cry. I asked

God over and over why? I felt like God broke his promise to me. So I began to give up on God and the Bible altogether.

I stopped going to church, and I stopped praying. I was angry at God for not answering my prayer. Nothing anyone could say would make me change my mind. From that day on everything the church taught me went out the window, and my faith was gone.

Chapter Eight

A Bitter Sweet Sixteen

At sixteen my life seemed to be spiraling out of control. I turned to alcohol whenever something was too hard for me to deal with. I found myself inebriated all the time. Thoughts of suicide were constantly on my mind. I just couldn't see myself living without James.

I wasn't mentally or emotionally stable the day of James' funeral. Mama refused to let me go, because she thought it would be too much for me to handle. My family went to have Thanksgiving dinner at our cousin's house, but I refused to go. So they left me at home alone.

My cousin Belinda and her boyfriend Reggie had introduced me to a boy name Ernest. I met him when I went to Belinda's house one weekend, and I knew he liked me. I went to the movies with him once when James and I were on a break and we talked on the phone, but it was nothing serious.

Ernest was tall, light skinned with green eyes and sandy brown hair. He was handsome, but he wasn't James. I was madly in love with James, and I couldn't see myself with anyone else.

Ernest knew James had died, and he asked if he could come over to try to cheer me up. I knew I was forbidden to let anyone in the house when my parents weren't home, but at the time I just didn't care about the rules.

When he arrived with his five year old niece I knew I had nothing to worry about. We put her in front of the television in the den, and we went in the living room and starting drinking gin and juice and smoking marijuana.

I must admit I was pretty drunk and high. Ernest and I sat there drinking, smoking and talking. We listened to some music then suddenly he started to kiss me. I must admit I liked it at first, until he started grabbing my breasts and trying to take off my clothes.

Ernest was about six feet two, and compared to me at five foot five, he looked like a giant. He kept trying to put his hands between my legs and beneath my blouse. I reminded him his niece was in the next room; figuring he would stop. He rose to his feet went into the den to find she was asleep.

Without warning he picked me, and carried me in my brother's bedroom. I didn't know what to do or what he was thinking.

He threw me on the tiny twin size bed with the Batman comforter on it, and without so much as a word he climbed on top on me. He tried to unbutton my pants, but I kept reaching for his hands in a gesture to stop.

He grabbed both of my arms, and held them over my head with one hand. He unbuttoned and unzipped my pants, and pulled them down around my ankles.

He pulled my panties to the side, and forced his huge penis inside me. He pounced on me like a wild animal, and all I could do was scream, "Please Stop! No! Don't!"

I kept shouting "I'm a virgin!" and the more I said no; the more he rammed his penis inside me, and each time it was harder and harder, as though the more I screamed for him to stop, the more excited he became.

I could feel something inside of me ripping, and it felt like someone was stabbing me with a knife. My entire body hurt all over. This went on for a while. He was moaning, and groaning; breathing hard and sweating profusely all over me. I could feel the moisture between my legs, and then as quickly as it began it ended.

He got up, walked into the tiny bathroom just steps away from my brother's bedroom. I could see him staring at himself in the mirror as though he was gloating.

He waited for the water to warm up, and then he spoke to me in a sarcastic tone of voice, and said, "You know you liked it". He found a towel, and washed himself off. He grabbed his keys, picked up his niece, and left.

I don't think he thought he did anything wrong. After all I welcomed him in; entertained and amused him, lead him on and aroused him, so why wouldn't he think I didn't want.

I thought to myself "That's what you get Raven". This was my fault. I knew better, but instead of doing what I was told to do, I did what I wanted to do, and this is what is cost me.

I laid there in a pool of blood for a few minutes, because I could barely move. The bottom half of my body was throbbing, my legs were shaking, and I was cover in his sweat and semen. I slowly got up; sat on the side of my brother's bed, and cried.

I carefully walked into the bathroom, looked at myself in the mirror with sheer disgust for what I'd allowed to happen to me, on the day of James' funeral.

My virginity was taken from me by someone I didn't even like, much less love. I got in the shower and tried to scrub the skin off my body because I felt so nasty and dirty.

I removed the sheets from the bed, only to see the mattress was stained with my blood. I flipped the mattress over to hide the imperfection. I had just started having my menstrual period a few months before my sixteenth birthday.

All my sisters started their period when they were eleven and twelve. Mama knew every time one of had our period, so if she saw blood on my little brother's mattress she'd suspect something. I knew if Mama found out, I would really be in big trouble.

After I washed the sheets I hung them on the clothes line in the back yard. I sat outside on the grass; looked in the sky and told James I was sorry for disappointing him, and that if I could take it back I would. I went back in the house, crawled into bed and went to sleep.

It was two am when I was awakened by my Mother; screaming and punching me. She said God showed her in a dream that I'd sex, and that I was going to be pregnant.

I tried persistently to tell her what happened, but she was in so much rage; she wouldn't listen. She looked at me amidst piercing eyes that seemed to cut through me like a knife. I'd always felt like the black sheep of the family anyway, and at that moment I knew she regretted even having me for a child.

For weeks mama, and daddy wouldn't speak to me; much less look at me. I felt like an unwanted intruder in my own home. My younger sisters Mia and Lisa made fun of me like they always did. They loved to see me get in trouble. My older sister Tina was the only one who tried to comfort me and give me advice.

I thought I had dodged a bullet because my period came for three months after that dreadful day, but as fate would have it, Mamas' prediction was right. In February 1979 just a few days after my seventeenth birthday, I found out I was pregnant.

I tried my best to hide the pregnancy from my family. I wore big clothes and coats in eighty degree weather. I avoided them as much as possible, until I could try to figure out what to do.

I was desperate for help so I called my friend Lana and told her everything. She came and picked me up and we drove around to search for Ernest.

We finally ran into him at a gas station in Inglewood. I told him I was pregnant. He looked at me and he laughed; then muttered something under his breath. Then in a sarcastic tone of voice he said; "How you know it's mine?"

I told him again that I was a virgin, and that I had never had sex with any other man. He laughed harder this time, and said "sure you were". I stood there crying, and humiliated as he degraded me in front of everyone.

Ernest looked at me with this cold look in his eyes and said; "you need to get an Abortion," as though it were as simple as a walk in the park. He didn't care about what he'd done to me, or the pain I was going through.

I told him I didn't have any money for an abortion, but that didn't seem to matter to him. He started up his engine, blasted his music and drove away; leaving me standing in the middle of the gas station feeling like a fool.

Ernest was in college; he had a good job with his father at an air craft plant. He drove a new car, wore nice clothes and had lots of money. His father and stepmother were well off. They lived in a safe, middle class neighborhood. In a beautiful house and they drove fancy cars too. Both his parents worked and made twice as much money as my father.

Ernest told me he would only give me half of the money to get the abortion. I didn't know what to do, so Lana took me to Planned Parenthood.

They wanted four hundred and fifty dollars to perform the abortion. I couldn't come up with one penny, so we went to the welfare office to apply for medical assistance; but all they did was give me a stack of papers, and told me to have my parents fill them out. I just threw them in the garbage, because I knew that would never happen.

I didn't have any way of getting the rest of the money. I knew if my parents found out they would never let me do it. Mama was a devoted Christian, who didn't believe in abortion.

I was so desperate, I tried to abort the baby myself by shoving a wire hanger into my vagina and some drinking bleach. Unfortunately; that did nothing but make me sick. The bleach made me throw up and the hanger caused an infection and made me bleed.

I could have died trying to abort the baby myself, but I was so afraid of what Mama and Daddy were going to do to me, that being dead seemed to be the easy way out.

It was March 1979; it was over eighty degrees in the Valley where my school was located. I wore a big winter coat to hide my enormous belly. Everyone looked at me strange and asked me why I had on a heavy coat. I lied and told them I had chills and that I didn't feel well.

By noon it was scorching outside. It had to be over ninety degrees. As I walked to the cafeteria I began to feel light headed and before I knew it I had passed out right in the courtyard.

I woke up in the nurses' office and she immediately asked me how many months pregnant I was. I tried to pretend that I didn't know what she was talking about, but it was clear by the bulge in my shirt, and the fact that I couldn't zip up my pants that I was pregnant.

The nurse called the principle; who called Mama. I was told I could no longer attend regular high school because of the nature of my medical condition and I was sent home.

I sat on the bus in silence thinking to myself "why me?" I was the one who never wanted children. They didn't fit into my plan. I walked home from the bus stop by myself that day, crying and trembling in fear of what mama was going to do to me. It was the longest walk of my life.

When I walked through the side door the house was quiet. My sisters and brother were still at school and daddy was at work. I could hear Mama in the kitchen cooking and singing like she always did. I was reluctant to go in her direction, so I went in my room; sat on the side of the bed and awaited my future.

A few minutes went by, and in comes Mama. Much to my amazement she wasn't mad. Instead, she held me in her arms, and we both cried together. My childhood was over, my virginity was gone. No more time for playing with Barbie's; now it was time to grow up, and be a woman; weather I wanted to or not.

I'd always dreamed that my first time would be beautiful; like a fairytale. My prince would rescue me, and sweep me off my feet. He'd wine and dine me, and shower me with gifts. I would be his queen and he would be my king.

He would proudly await, as I pranced down the aisle in my beautiful white designer wedding dress; stepping on rose petals along the way.

I would glide to the altar, and become his wife. He would carry me into our hotel suite on a beautiful sandy beach in the Bahamas, and in our heart shaped bed we would make love until the sun came up, and live happily ever after.

I guess I'd read too many of my sisters' romance novels. My dream quickly turned in to a nightmare. The happily ever after I envisioned for my future was quickly erased, and now I had to live with the consequences of my mistakes.

Chapter Nine

Life Just Got Real

It's August 1979; I was nine months pregnant. I had gained sixty pounds, and I looked as though I was ready to explode. I didn't know what having a baby would feel like, but I knew from the films we saw in maternity school that it was going to be painful.

I never understood why people called sex "making love", because it didn't feel good to me at all. I couldn't imagine having a baby come out of that tiny little hole, but I was sure that it was going to hurt more than having sex.

My friends gave me a baby shower that beautiful Sunday afternoon. All the members of the church came; we played games, ate lunch, and they brought me lovely gifts for the baby.

When I got home later that night, I was craving fried chicken and a jalapeno pepper, so Mama went to get it for me, and no sooner as I took a bite of my chicken it happened.

A pain shot through my body like a bullet. All I could do was scream for Mama! Then it came again and again. Before I knew it something was leaking out of me. I thought I had urinated on myself, so I wobbled to the bathroom to see what was wrong.

Just as I sat down on the toilet this sharp pain came again only more intense. Mama came in the bathroom with a watch and started to time the pains, then she informed me I was in labor.

When the contractions started coming every five minutes she put me in the car, and drove me to the hospital. They wheeled me into the emergency room, and immediately put me in a bed.

Mama was right there by my side every step of the way; holding my hand and telling me to breathe. I didn't bother to call Ernest because I knew he didn't care. I ran into him a few times after I got pregnant and he'd promise that he was going to help me take care of the baby but he never did anything.

As far as I was concerned he was just a sperm donor, who stole my virginity and left me with an unwanted baby. It was obvious he didn't care about me much less the baby, and I knew he wouldn't come to the hospital so I didn't bother calling him.

The nurse strapped what looked to be a big belt around my stomach with a huge buckle. The nurse told me it would monitor the contractions.

Every time I looked at the monitor I could see when another contraction was coming. It was so terrifying; the anguish was unbearable, and for a while I just wanted to die, because I didn't think I could handle the pain another second.

It was the hardest twenty-four hours of my life, and it hurt far more than I had ever imagined. Every part of my body was aching. My back hurt; my stomach felt like I had cramps, and my feet were swollen the size of grapefruits.

This went on for hours and hours; I was about to give up any hope of survival when the doctor finally came in. The nurse put my legs in stirrups, and made me slide down to the end of the bed.

The doctor put his big cold hands inside me, and announced that I had dilated ten centimeters. He advised me to push, and I pushed as hard as I could, but nothing happened. He kept saying "try again", and after five or six times I suddenly felt relief and the pain was gone.

I heard the sound of a baby cry, and I looked up; and there she was, this beautiful baby girl. She weighed six pounds, three ounces, and she was twenty-one inches long. She had a head full of cold black hair and her skin was so light she could pass for white.

They laid her on my chest, and she opened her eyes and looked at me. She was the spitting image of Ernest. If I hadn't just given birth to her myself I wouldn't believe she was mine. She looked nothing like me.

Mama and I were both in tears. The nurse took her away to clean her up, and suddenly the reality started to sink in that I was a mother. What was I going to do now? I had no clue of how to take care of a baby; I was still playing with dolls when I got pregnant.

I was released from the hospital after a week. My baby was ill so, they kept her in the hospital. The doctor said she had jaundice. I didn't know what that was; all I knew was she was kept in an incubator under a bright light with blind folds over her eyes for over a month.

They shaved her hair off in the front of her head, and placed needles in it. I felt so sorry for this tiny little creature. I know it must have hurt, but there was nothing I could do to help her.

Mama and I would go up to the hospital every day and sit for hours. I was scared to hold her because she was so small, so Mama cradled her in her one good arm, and rocked her to sleep every day.

When it was time for her to come home, I was so afraid and overwhelmed that I fell into a deep depression. The thought of being an unwed teenage mother was not what I anticipated for myself. Everything I'd ever dreamed of for my future was now a distant memory. I was responsible for someone else's' life now, and I didn't even know how to take care of myself.

In my mind my life was over before it began. It didn't help that the baby looked just like him! She was the mirror image of him. It made me sad every time I looked at her; she was supposed to be James' baby. I felt so guilty, like I cheated on James by getting pregnant the day of his funeral; and to add insult to injury having a baby by a man I didn't really know or love.

At first I lied and told people the baby might be James' because I was too embarrassed to tell anyone the truth. After all it was my fault, if I hadn't let him in or led him on, this wouldn't have happened. I would have to live with this mistake for rest of my existence, and the guilt began to eat away at me like cancer.

My mental state of mind was that of a child. I didn't know the first thing about being somebody's mama, or taking care of a baby. She was like a doll to me. I would dress her up; brush her hair, and just stare at her as though she wasn't real.

I tried to get up at night to feed and change her, but she would just cry endlessly as though I was hurting her, so Mama would get up every night, and as soon as she held her she stopped crying.

I started to think the baby didn't like me, or maybe she could feel that she was unwanted. Eventually Mama moved the baby into her room, and took care of her every night so I could sleep, because I had to go to school.

Mama kept her every day while I was at school and soon she was calling my mother "Mama". It didn't bother me because she was more like a sister to me than a daughter.

Ernest was nowhere to be found, his parents came by once to see the baby and brought her gifts, but for the most part he was not a part of her life. Every now and then I'd run into him on the streets, and he'd ask about her as if she was a puppy or some kind of toy you just leave behind.

He was never a real father to her, my father played that role. Mama was thirty-four and Daddy was thirty-six when they became parents again.

I loved my baby the best way I knew how, but I just wasn't ready for the responsibility. I could barely take care of myself much less another human being. I just wanted to run as far away as I could; disappear and become someone else.

I had no job or money and nowhere to go. I was still in high school and I was still a child. I turned to alcohol even more to escape reality. I was drunk and high more than I was sober.

I was so lost, and confused that I even tried to have a relationship with Ernest even though I hated him, because I thought it would be better to be with my baby's daddy then to be alone.

Ernest was mean, and evil. He treated me like I was nothing. He'd even slapped and choked me a few times just for being in his neighborhood without his permission.

He quit his job to avoid paying child support, and decided to become a thug. He stole cars, sold drugs and eventually joined a gang. He was rotten to the core. He got what he wanted from me, and then treated me and our baby like Alabama trash.

Ernest made me feel like I was worthless. He bragged to his friends about how he took my virginity. I felt like everyone looked down on me, and even if they really didn't; in my mind I thought they did. I felt like God stopped loving me, and that I was being punished for my sins.

I was running around like a chicken with its head cut off. I wore a fake smile like costume jewelry, and I laughed and made jokes when

I was dying inside.

Where I grew up going to college was rare, most of the kids barely completed high school. I had become a product of my environment, a statistic; the one thing I didn't want to become.

My dreams of college were just that; a dream. I became indigent; I thought I needed a man to love me, and I needed friends to accept me. I don't know why I thirsted for so much attention, all I knew was I could not be alone very long because the thought of failure would consume me, and all I felt about my life was doom and gloom.

I had given up on life at seventeen. While I was at home stuck with a baby, Ernest was out living his life, and having fun. He got to be a teenager while I was stuck being a mother. I despised him and often wished death on him for destroying my life!

Ernest had a step-sister named Aliyah. I met her when I was pregnant, and we immediately hit it off. I think it was because she didn't have any sisters, and was very lonely.

Aliyah was short and a little chubby. She had beautiful cold black wavy hair, flawless bronze skin and a huge smile. She was loud, and boisterous and loved to drink and have fun.

She stuck to me like glue, and although she was younger than me; she was very mature. She didn't like the way Ernest treated me or the baby.

One summer Aliyah came to visit for a weekend, and never left. She stayed the entire summer. I admired Aliyah because she was a hustler, and she was down for anything. I knew I could trust her, and that she had my back.

We had our ups and downs like most friends do, but for the most part, I knew she loved me like the sister she never had, and she looked up to me which I could never understand.

Aliyah had four older brothers who she really loved, and she tried to have a close relationship with them, but they ignored her most of the time, and treated her like she was invisible.

When she was fifteen she got a job with a fake identification card and social security number and worked for months. She saved every penny, and brought a car without her parents' knowledge. She had the car for months before they found out.

She would pick me up and we'd gather all our friends together, get some liquor and head to the beach. We did everything together. She was my rock, and she didn't even know it.

Everything she had she shared it with me. We shared many secrets and dreams. She was truly genuine and I trusted her with my life. One day Aliyah and I went to the liquor store to buy some wine coolers. This was the first time mama let me take my baby anywhere because she didn't trust my friends or my judgment and she had every reason no too.

We pulled up in front of the store located in south central Los Angeles and there were several drunks loitering in front. I didn't think much of it because that's all they did in my neck of the woods.

We went in the store brought the wine and headed for the car. When we walked outside everyone had scattered. I thought that was strange, but I walked towards the car, and just as I put my hand on the door handle; two men came for nowhere pointing guns in our faces.

They demanded the keys and our jewelry and purses, but Aliyah refused. The man shoved the gun in the back of her head and yelled at her to give him the keys and again she refused.

I pleaded with her to give them the keys and finally she did. I grabbed my baby and tried to run but the man pointing the gun at me told the other man to take me with him.

I begged him not to take me. I was crying and holding my baby as tight as I could, and finally the driver said lets go and they jumped in the car and took off leaving us standing in the cold.

That was the first, and the last time mama let me take the baby anywhere for a long time, and I didn't blame her one bit.

God spared my life once again, and I was grateful for that.

Chapter Ten

The Tears Behind My Smile

It was my senior year; my parents were determined to see me walk across the stage and get my diploma. I dreaded going back to traditional high school because I knew the word had gotten out that I'd a baby, and I knew that people would judge me. At the maternity school, I fit in because everyone was just like me; unwed, pregnant teenagers.

Going back to high school was hard, the girls were cruel and treated me like trash. I could feel the tension and see the girls staring at me as I walked down the hallway or sat in the classroom. All the boys thought I was easy because I had a baby, and the one time I did get asked out on a date the boy took me to the drive-in and tried to have sex with me in the back seat of his Camaro.

I tried to keep him off me, by hitting him between his legs, and he kicked me out of the car. I ended up walking to a phone booth to call my daddy to pick me up. I didn't date anyone for a long time after that. I didn't have many friends because every time I trusted someone they betrayed me, they smiled in my face and talked about me behind my back. I always tried to buy friends, because I didn't think people would like me if I came empty handed.

Once in my senior year of high school I applied for a Montgomery Ward credit card. I had no job and everything on the application was made up, but somehow they sent it to me anyway.

It had a five hundred dollar limit. I'd never had that much money in my entire life. I couldn't wait to use it, but I didn't know how. I told some girls in my gym class about it, and they told me if I brought them something they'd would show me how to use it.

The next day I ditched school and met the girls whom I thought were my friends at the Hawthorne Mall, and we went on a shopping spree.

We spent every dime on clothes, shoes and makeup. The next day when I got to school they wouldn't even speak to me. I felt like such a fool when they walked right pass me in the hallway laughing. The sad part was we were all wearing the same outfit, and from that day on I kept to myself.

It was towards the end of the twelfth grade when I met a boy named Roger. He seemed harmless, and he always smiled at me and had nice things to say. I really begin to like him because he wasn't loud and obnoxious like the other boys; he was quiet and sweet.

He took me to the movies a few times and to the park. He never tried to get between my legs and that's what I liked about him the most. He accepted my daughter, and every time he picked me up for a date he'd always bring a gift for her.

Roger wasn't fine like James. He was an average looking boy with a light complexion, thin mustache and a gap in his front teeth.

He had a big afro, and he was short. Roger stood about five feet seven, and when I put on heels I was taller them him so I wore flats most of the time.

I don't know if I liked him or if I was just desperate for attention. Roger was the only boy hanging around who didn't seem to want anything from me, so when he asked me to the prom I accepted. I couldn't wait to get home to tell mama the good news.

After school I stopped at the grocery store and stole some magazines so I could find the perfect dress. I loved to draw and I had a notebook with sketches and designs of what my wedding dress would look like one day.

When I told Mama she was so happy for me, and she promised to help me find a dress.

Mama and I went everywhere trying to find a picture-perfect gown. It was hard to find a dress because I had champagne taste on a beer budget. I asked mama to take me to Beverly Hills, but she refused, so I caught the bus. I'd seen ads about Saks Fifth Avenue in cosmopolitan magazine, and I just had to go. When I got off the bus on Wilshire Blvd, it was like I had died and gone to fashion heaven. It was like nothing I'd even seen. The streets were clean, there was no bums walking around begging for money or no drunks standing on the corner smelling of urine. It was simply beautiful.

The buildings looked like art. Which was a far cry from the Kmart I was used to in South Central Los Angeles. The air even smelled different.

I walked into Saks Fifth Avenue and as the doors opened I could hear beautiful music playing in the distance as though it was a concert. When I reached the middle of the lobby there was a man wearing a black tuxedo playing a baby grand piano.

I was in awe to say the least. I had always dreamed that one day I'd be rich enough to shop in an elegant store like Saks. I didn't know where to begin; everything I saw caught my eyes. Then I realized the sales clerks were staring at me, and following me around the store. I guess they assumed by the color of my skin and the way I was dressed that I was going to steal something.

As I browsed through the formal gowns, I noticed there were no prices on the tags; only bar codes. I picked out a few dresses and headed for the fitting room. The clerk took my dresses, counted them, then she walked me to the back and opened the door to the elegant fitting room. I tried on three of the most beautiful dresses I'd ever seen.

I narrowed it down to one; a beautiful coral fitted evening gown with spaghetti straps. I went to the cashier to find out the price, and the clerk looked at me as if I was beneath her, and in a nonchalant voice she said "it's on sale for five hundred and ninety-five dollars."

I stood there for a few seconds pretending to still be interested. I asked the clerk if I could put the dress on layaway and she nearly choked as she informed me that they didn't do layaway. That was the last I'd seen of that dress, and Saks Fifth Avenue. I walked to the bus stop, sat on the bench to wait for my bus and cried all the way home. I loathed being poor.

A few weeks went by and I still hadn't found anything that I liked and could afford. I finally had to settle for a dress that Mama picked out at J.C. Penney. It wasn't nearly as beautiful as the dress from Saks. As a matter of fact I detested it. It was an off white dress with sequence on the top, and a short jacket. It looked like something an old lady would wear. It only cost twenty-five dollars on clearance, and since time was running out I was forced to get it.

I called Roger to tell him I'd finally found a dress so he could pick out his tuxedo and cummerbund to match, but he wasn't home and he didn't call back.

I called every day for a week straight, and every time I called his house his mother or sister's would say he wasn't home. It was clear to me that Roger had changed his mind about taking me to the prom.

I was heartbroken; I couldn't understand for the life of me what happened or why Roger didn't even have the decency to tell me himself.

It was May 1980 just a few days before the prom. I still hadn't seen or heard from Roger, he made a point of avoiding me at school too, so I'd made up my mind that I wasn't going to the prom.

Mama convinced me to swallow my pride; hold my head up and go anyway. I mentioned to my friend Edward that I didn't have a date and because he was gay he hadn't planned on going because people frowned on gay relationships.

Edward felt so sorry for me he offered to take me to the prom. He didn't have time to rent a tuxedo so he wore a brown suit and cream strip tie to match my dress. I washed the tears off my face; took a bath, got dressed and went to the prom alone.

Edward picked me up in his father's burgundy Cadillac. It was the best looking car in the world, but it beat riding the bus or having daddy take us.

I was too embarrassed for him to pull up in front of the lavish Westin Bonaventure hotel so I made him park a few blocks away. We walked into the extravagant Hotel side by side, while all the other girls were hand and hand with their escorts.

We sat down at a table in the back of the ballroom and watched as the room filled with prom dresses and tuxedos.

The band was playing, and people smiling were dancing. Suddenly I heard a familiar voice coming from behind me, I turned to see Roger standing there holding hands with Jasmine.

Roger told me they'd broken up months before he met me. My heart sank to the floor. I could feel the tears welling up in my eyes, but I fought to keep them from rolling down my cheeks. Our eyes met briefly; then he put his head down, and walked away.

I stood next to the wall most of the night watching as everyone danced and posed for pictures. I was humiliated to say the least, but I refused to let him or anyone else know it.

I went into the bathroom, and sat in the stall and smoked a joint. Marijuana always made me feel relaxed; like nothing mattered. I walked out on the dance floor and Edward and I danced until our feet hurt.

I pretended I was having a good time because I couldn't give him the satisfaction of knowing just how bad he'd really hurt me. When the night came to an end, Edward and I went to breakfast and then he dropped me off at home. Meanwhile all the other couples went to an all-night bonfire at the beach or to the motel. I had planned in my mind that I was going to give myself to Roger but I guess it wasn't meant to be.

I found out later that Roger's mother had forbidden him to see me or take me to the prom. At first I didn't understand why, but then I learned that his mother didn't like me because I had a baby. I was constantly being judged by everyone, so I wasn't surprised.

Graduation day came, and I was glad high school was finally over. Roger was persistent; he kept calling after graduation, telling me how sorry he was.

I guess loneliness made me do foolish things, so eventually I forgave Roger. I convinced myself that it was his mother's fault he stood me up for the prom.

At least that's what I told everyone else to justify my decision for taking him back. Roger and I hung out the entire summer, and I didn't realize for quite some time that he was sneaking around with me behind his Mother's back.

I got a job as a cashier at Kmart department store after graduation. Roger had a job working with his father. He professed his undying love for me, and asked me to marry him, and have his baby. He promised he would never hurt me again. I was so stupid and naïve I agreed.

We had sex every chance we could and in my childish little mind

I really thought I was ready to have another child, and that Roger really was going to marry me. I started looking for apartments in the newspaper, and I even put household items on layaway.

I bragged to my sister's that I was moving out, and getting married. A few months later I found out I was pregnant. I was happy this time because everything was going as planned, or so I thought.

I told Roger that we needed to tell his mother Joann the good news. I knew she didn't like me because I had a baby, but I thought she'd have to accept me now, because I was going to marry her son, and have his child.

Joann was very intimidating. She was loud and obnoxious, and didn't sugar coat anything. She was high yellow, with sandy brown shoulder length hair, and freckles. Roger looked just like his mother, and he was her first born, and I could see that she was very protective over him.

She stood about five-feet six and had a medium build. She had a raspy voice, and she was straight forward and to the point. Roger was nothing like his mother. He was weak and timid.

When we walked in the house everyone became silent. You could hear a rat piss on cotton. I walked over to the dining room table where Joann was sitting.

There were a house full of family members there, and I asked his mother if I could talk to her in private. She told me to say what I needed to say right there, so I blurted out that I was pregnant by Roger and that we were getting married.

If looks could kill; I would have dropped dead! She took a large gulp of her Crown Royal and calmly said; "Over my dead body" along with other choice words!

She said I was nothing more than a whore, and a slut trying to trap her son with a baby. Roger just stood there like a coward and said nothing to defend me. That's when I realized he was nothing more than a Mama's boy.

We left his mother's house that evening right before she threatened to throw me threw her picture window. She made of point of letting me know that if the baby did turn out to be Roger's she was going to take it from me, because she felt I was unfit. I knew then that I'd made another poor judgment call by trusting Roger again.

It didn't take long for him to show his true colors either. The further along I got in my pregnancy the less I saw of him. I was six months pregnant when I found out that Roger had been cheating with the same girl he took to the prom. To add insult to injury she was pregnant by him too.

I nearly had a nervous breakdown. I stayed in bed and cried for weeks. I couldn't eat or sleep, all I knew was I was having another bastard child out of wedlock by a sorry ass boy!

A few weeks passed when the clinic called, and told me I needed to come in right away; they said it was urgent. The doctor informed me that I'd contracted a sexually transmitted disease and that it was in the third stage. He said the Gonorrhea was so severe that my baby could be born blind, deaf or mentally retarded.

The doctor then informed me that Roger had to know that he had it, because the symptoms in men appeared within three days, and is a burning painful urination, and bodily fluids leaking from his penis.

What hurt me the most was that Roger didn't even have the guts to tell me? I was treated with antibiotics for several weeks; abortion wasn't an option at six months pregnant; so there was nothing I could do but wait until my baby was born and pray that it was healthy.

My psychological state of mind was worsening. My will to live was gone. There I was; nineteen, un-wed, with one child and another on the way.

On a cold, dreary October day in 1981; my second child was born. She had beaten all the odds, and was healthy and beautiful. God had worked a miracle, yet I found myself in a worst position than before, with two kids, on welfare; alone.

I found out later that the other girl Roger got pregnant had an abortion. In my mind she made the right choice, and I made the wrong one. I didn't know whether to be happy or sad, because I realized I was stuck with another baby with no father.

In my eyes Roger was worst then Ernest. At least Ernest never made any false promises or pretended to love me or our child. Roger came in and out of our life numerous times; making false promises to me and our daughter each and every time, and out of desperation

I took him back.

Although he portrayed the cowardly role with his mother, Roger had his demons too, and when he drank; he became abusive. Once he attacked me in front of our daughter, slapping and choking me, as she stood there screaming for him to stop.

I endured his cycle of physical, and mental abuse, because I didn't want to raise another child alone, but Roger eventually choose drugs over me, and our child. He devoted his life to the streets and getting high. He became a full-fledged crack head at the age of twenty-two.

Things had gotten so bad that he had to leave the state because he owed drug dealers thousands of dollars. He moved to the east coast, and I didn't see or hear from him for several years.

He never sent our daughter any gifts for Christmas, or birthday's. He never attended any school functions, and the children in the neighborhood, and at school thought that my daddy was my kids' father too.

When he finally did resurface, he had a new family. A white chick with two kids calling him Daddy, and although Roger's mother didn't seem to like me very much; she loved, and adored our daughter Monica, and was a wonderful grandmother to her.

I was so afraid that his mother would try to take her from me, I didn't put his name on the birth certificate. Instead I put Ernest name on it because I knew he'd never try to take her away from me.

Joann played the role her son failed to play in his daughter's life. She provided for her, spoiled her rotten, and loved her unconditionally.

I realized although she was abrasive on the surface with me, deep down; she was a loving, caring woman; who loved her children like my mother loved us.

I recognized that Joann wasn't mean or evil, she just saw thru my disguise, and she knew when to call a spade a spade. I had an unspoken love, and respect for her, and although she never said it, I knew she loved me too, in her own way.

As time went on I became bitter. I began to despise men altogether. Their promises became void to me, and soon I built a wall around myself that no one could penetrate. I knew the only man I could ever trust was my father, so I gave up on love.

I wondered how Mama got Daddy to love her so much. They got married so young, had five children by the time they were in their mid-twenties and Daddy never left us. Even when Mama was sick in the hospital for years; he worked his fingers to the bone to pay the hospital bills, and stayed by her side never complaining once. I always wanted a man like my father, but that just wasn't in the cards for me.

Chapter Eleven

Sex, Drugs, and Everything in Between

It was New Year's Eve 1982; I was twenty years old, and wild as could be. My cousin Patricia, and I went to a club called the Carolina West. She helped me get a fake identification card to get in; because the age limit was twenty-one and over.

The club was located on Century Blvd near LAX airport. It was one of the hottest clubs in town, and it sat next to an adult book store. I could see all the weird looking men going in to watch the peep shows while we was standing in line.

The parking lot was filled with nice expensive cars and the club was packed with fine men, dressed from head to toe. You could spot the men with money sitting in the VIP section, trying to look important.

Everyone was drinking, smoking and socializing. The music was blasting as we made our way into the club. We found a small table and sat for a few minutes waiting for a waitress to come take our drink order. I'd never been to a club before, and I was amazed at how some of the women were dressed.

Most of them looked like prostitutes, with their breast hanging out; short skirts and stilettos. They left nothing to the imagination.

My cousin Patricia was a year older than me, and much worldlier. She was very attractive and seductive. She had this sexy walk that would turn heads.

She was high yellow, with smooth honey colored skin, dark brown eyes and sandy brown hair. She had a smile that could charm the savage beast, and she knew how to get a man to do whatever she wanted. She told me to let her do all the talking because I didn't even know how to order a drink.

I lit a cigarette, and waited patiently for the waitress to return. We both knew it was going to take a while for the drinks to come because the place was so packed, so Patricia, and I decided to walk around to scope out potential targets.

We made our way to the bathroom, the line was long, but Patricia wanted to wait. When we finally got in I saw a stall door opened so headed toward it, and there sat a white girl on the toilet. She had this white powder placed in some foil on her lap, and people were rolling up twenty dollar bills and sniffing it up their nose. I was always adventurous and vowed I would try everything at least once before I died.

I must admit I was a little scared, so Patricia grabbed the twenty dollar bill and inhaled. She said it felt good, so I took the rolled up twenty dollar bill, and inhaled too. I could feel my heart beating a mile a minute.

I began to breathe hard and sweat profusely. Then my body began to tingle all over. I'd never felt anything like that before. It was an exhilarating feeling that took me away. It made me feel sexy, and beautiful. I asked Patricia what it was, and she informed me I'd just tried cocaine.

We danced, and partied all night long. I was so drunk, and high I couldn't remember what else we did or didn't do. I don't even know who drove us home. All I remember is waking up the next day in the back seat of my Patricia's car; half un-dressed, hung-over, and high as a kite.

Patricia was wild, and crazy like me, and whenever we got together there were no limits what she would do. Even I had boundaries but Patricia walked on the wild side and took chances that scared even me!

I couldn't wait for the summer, because she'd always come stay with us. We were bad for each other because we never talked each other out of doing anything wrong.

Once we took some L.S.D. I didn't know what it was at the time. It just looked like a dried up piece of paper. She told me to stick it under my tongue, and suck on it, and like a fool I did it.

The next thing I knew; I started seeing flying monkeys, and Mickey Mouse. I started perspiring, and hallucinating. My mouth felt as dry as the Mohave Desert; like I'd drank a glass full of sand.

It took hours for me to come down off that drug, and I vowed I'd never try that again. We took so many chances with our lives, because we thought life was a joke.

Patricia, and I were pregnant at the same time. Her son was a few months younger than my second daughter Monica. What was ironic, was that her baby's daddy Stephen was close friends with Roger.

Stephen was in her child's life, and he took good care of her, and their baby. I was jealous of my cousin Patricia, because she seemed to have it all, while I had nothing.

She was beautiful; confident, sexy, and intelligent. I loved being around her because she had that I don't give a damn attitude. Whenever a man would hurt me she'd tell me to go get a new one; as though they were a pair of old shoes.

Her nonchalant personality was something I truly admired, because if something or someone really did hurt her; she definitely didn't show it. She would dismiss a man as quickly as she would say hello. I wish I had the strength to do that.

None of the men in my life ever gave me anything, but grief, and I accepted it like it was a gift. I often wondered how it would feel to treat a man the way they treated me.

To leave him high, and dry with a baby, to lie, and cheat on him all the time, and beat him until he was black and blue. I wanted to be anyone but myself. I was weak; my self-esteem was non-existent, and I felt useless, and men could sense it.

I couldn't keep a man unless I allowed them to walk all over me like a rug, and most of the time they did. Patricia made me feel like I was worth something, and even though most of the time we were drunk, or high on something, we always managed to make the best of a bad situation.

My parents got tired of me running the streets, partying all the time. They informed me I had to get my act together, or get out. A month later I moved into a two bedroom apartment on the other side of town with a roommate.

At first I tried to take my kids with me out of spite; but Mama would go to hell and back before she let that happened. She refused to let them go, and threatened to call Child Protective Services if I tried to take them.

At first I pretended to be angry, but I knew it was for the best. After all I wasn't fit to be a mother; I liked to party all the time; run the streets, drink, and use drugs.

I cared more about having fun then I did about being a mother. They didn't fit in my plans at the time, and I knew it was best that they stayed with my parents anyway; if they ever wanted a chance in life.

I loved them the best way I knew how. I always made sure they had the best clothes, and shoes, and that they didn't want for any- thing.

I treated them like dolls, because in my immature mind that's what they were to me. I found myself constantly wishing this was all a bad dream, and that I'd wake up and be fifteen again with no children, and no responsibility.

I didn't realize at the time that all they wanted, and needed was me, but I would find out later in life that I sacrificed the best love of my life, and it was all for nothing.

My apartment was the kick it spot. Everyone gathered there to get high, drunk, and have sex. My roommate was a short, fat slut who slept with anyone willing to give her a drink, or drugs.

I wasn't any better. I was a friendly drunk; who'd buy all the liquor, feed everybody, and give away everything I had just to have friends around because I hated to be alone.

I didn't have morals or values. I'd let any man who claimed they liked me move in and get between my legs. It didn't matter who it was as long as I had someone to talk to. I knew they were using me, but it didn't matter; I was accustom to being used, and I didn't expect anything more.

I didn't value my life, or what I was doing to my family. My actions were those of someone on a suicide mission; then Crack Cocaine hit my neighborhood hard, and before I knew it I found myself caught up on the band wagon.

I started lacing my cigarettes with crack cocaine, because I thought it was cool; then I started smoking it in a glass pipe. I loved the way it made me feel; as though I was in a dream floating high above the clouds.

Coke made me do things that I never thought I'd ever do. I was pawning and selling anything I could get my hands on. My roommate and I spent the rent money, and sold our food stamps just to get high. It didn't matter if her kid had anything to eat.

I knew it wouldn't be long before I sold my body because the drug was that addicting. I wanted to experience that high all the time and no matter how much I smoked I could never get that feeling again.

I knew it was getting out of control. It got so bad where I lived; that my neighborhood started to resemble the night of the living dead. Everyone started to look like zombies, running around looking for crack.

People who were once friends were robbing, and stealing from each other just to get high. We would all gather in an apartment, and smoke crack together all day and night and when it was all gone; you'd hear people screaming, and fighting to smoke the residue left at the bottom of the pipe.

We'd crawl around on the ground searching for rocks like bloodhounds. It was like a science fiction movie. One day I glanced at myself in the mirror after a long night of partying, and the person that looked back at me was a stranger.

I was killing myself, and didn't even care. I stood there staring at the reflection in the mirror. Then I heard a voice in my head say "you're worthless, nobody loves you; you should just kill yourself, and put everyone out of their misery."

I washed down a bottle of pain pills with some gin, and went to sleep. There was no suicide note, no good byes; nothing, I just wanted life to be over.

I don't know who found me, or how. When I awoke; I was in a mental hospital. They'd branded me 51/50. I was lying in bed, dazed out of my mind. The psychiatrist came in, and sat next to the bed; he spoke calmly; almost monotone.

He asked me why I tried to kill myself, and I told him I was tired of living. He took a deep breath, stared down at my chart; looked at me, and said "You haven't lived yet". I stayed there for three days; attended several group meetings, and had a one on one session with a counselor.

I put on my mask like I often did, and convinced them I was alright, and that I was going to get my life together. I told them whatever they wanted to hear; because lying came easy to me, it was something I did without some much as a thought.

I had to get out of there; I needed a drink, and a cigarette bad. The doctor walked me to the door; he looked at me as though he could see right through me, and said; "Look around you; you're not like these people, go do something with your life".

I did go home that day; but that didn't last long, my parents had guidelines that I just refused to follow, so I found myself back on the streets again, but by choice this time.

I got crack on credit, convincing the dude that gave it to me that I was going to sell it. I ended up smoking all three ounces and the word was out that he was looking for me to kill me. I didn't have anywhere to go or anyone I could trust so I ran to mama and daddy like I usually did when I was in trouble. They scraped up the money to buy me a plane ticket to Louisiana and sent me to stay with my grandmother.

I stayed there six months until things blew over and I got myself together. I made a promise to myself that I would never use crack, and I would not put my parents in that position again.

When I got home, I was in, and out of hospitals a lot. I suffered from a chronic kidney disease, and female problems. It didn't help that I drank alcohol while taking the antibiotics, so the infection never ceased in my body. I didn't get regular checkups either. I'd wear my body down until I could go no further. Then end up hospitalized; needing intravenous antibiotics, and fluids.

I guess it didn't help my body by having multiple abortions. I'd gotten three by the time I was twenty one. Several doctors told me it was likely that I couldn't have any more children; which was fine with me.

I'd let men destroy my body, because I felt lucky they'd even want me in the first place. Sexual intercourse was always painful for me, but I learned to endure it with alcohol, and drugs.

I'd never experienced that wonderful feeling other girls were talking about when they had sex. I often wondered if I was the only person cursed with this numbness. I longed to enjoy the pleasure that everyone else experienced. I yearned to feel what making love felt like. I wanted to cry tears of joy afterwards; instead of tears of pain, but it never happened.

Sex was like a job that I hated to go to. Sometimes I would be in the hospital for weeks at a time, because my female organs were infected, and inflamed from the abuse a man put on my body.

My friends would come up to the hospital bearing gifts of liquor, and marijuana. We'd get drunk, and high in the hospital room while the antibiotics were being pumped through my veins.

I abused pain pills, and would mix them with alcohol to get a better high. The doctors wrote me off a few times, telling me that at the rate I was going; I'd be lucky to live to see thirty.

One day I was driving on the freeway when I suddenly I found myself doubled over in pain. I veered off into the emergency lane to avoid an accident. The pain was so severe I could hardly move.

I sat there for a while before a passing motorist stopped to see if I needed help. When he looked at me his face said it all. I had the look of death. A few moments later highway patrolman arrived, and called an ambulance.

I was transported to Harbor General Hospital. I awakened two days later, and I found myself in Intensive care. The doctor's said I was severely dehydrated, and that my right kidney was infected and my liver was enlarged.

I wasn't surprised by the diagnosis, considering I come from a long line of alcoholics. It was as if it was a generational curse. My uncle dropped dead in my grandmother's house at the age of forty from liver failure, and I was sure I was going to die the same way.

The infection spread throughout my body into my blood stream. It was so bad that everyone had to put on sterile hospital clothing, masks, and gloves.

My immune system was so low; a common cold could kill me. I had been there for several weeks, and they couldn't get the infection under control. The doctor's told me that my chances of survival were slim. I'd done so much damage to myself; that my body wasn't strong enough to fight anymore. I'd given up, and was ready to accept death, because I was tired.

My mother came to see me every day like clockwork. She'd bring her Bible, and her anointing oil; lay hands on me, and pray. I always believed mama had a gift of healing so whenever she prayed for me, no matter how bad the doctor's said it was, I didn't worry. That night before my mother left; several doctors came into my room, and told us the grim news.

They felt there was nothing else they could do. My fever wouldn't break; my blood pressure was high, and the numerous antibiotics they'd tried did nothing. I was at the end of my rope, but mama had a smile on her face. She looked at the doctors, and said; "Well I'm just going to trust in the Lord". She looked at me, told me to repent of my sins, and trust God. She kissed me on the cheek, and left.

That night I was afraid to sleep; fearing that I was going to die. In the middle of the night I was awakened by a male nurse. He was dressed in all white; standing at the end of my bed reading my chart.

He looked at me; smiled, and didn't say a word. He placed his hands gently on my feet; on top of the blanket, and held them there for a few minutes, then he walked out the room. I went back to sleep thinking nothing of it. The next morning when I had awakened, my fever had broken. My blood pressure was normal, and my pain was gone.

When the nurse came in to take my vital signs; she was shocked. I asked her what happened to the male nurse that came into my room last night. She looked at me rather strangely, and said there was no male nurse on duty last night. She thought I must have been dreaming, but I knew it wasn't a dream, because I recalled his face and I remembered his touch.

He was a young white man with long brown hair; brown eyes, and a warm smile. When the doctor's came they were amazed at my progress. The doctor said it was nothing short of a miracle, and he was right. God had worked a miracle, and sent an angel to heal me. A week later I was released.

Chapter Twelve

Selling Myself a Dream

I wanted more out of life than just a welfare check. I couldn't survive off four hundred, and twenty-seven dollars a month, and I didn't have a man to help me. All they did was take what little I had, I was tired of using drugs and making the dope dealers rich so that's when I decided to start selling drugs.

I took two hundred dollars; which was all the money I had in the world, so I brought some powdered cocaine. Instead of rocking it up for me and my free loading friends to smoke; I weigh it and packaged it for sale. I put each rock of cocaine in tiny little zip lock bags, and that's when it all begin.

I sold the crack within a couple of hours, and doubled my money. As soon as I sold out I brought some more. I was up for three days, and night's non-stop, because people wouldn't stop coming. I started to get scared that someone would snitch, because that's what crack heads do.

I knew I had to get out of that neighborhood if I wanted to make real money. I used an alias and called myself "Lacy" and moved to Inglewood, which was only a few miles west of where I lived. I moved into an apartment across the street from Morningside high school.

The neighborhood was infested with drugs, but I wasn't intimidated at all. I was one of the few women bold enough to sell drugs on the streets, so the guys showed me respect, and would look out for me from time to time.

I knew I needed protection, so I purchased a gun from someone on the streets for three hundred dollars. It was a cute little pearl handle twenty-two, and I never left home without it.

I started selling drugs in front of my apartment building until one of the crack heads found out where I lived, and tried to break in.

I moved to a corner within walking distance from where I lived to sell dope, because I didn't have a car at the time. I'd stay up sometimes for days curb serving crack cocaine on the streets. I was determined to get rich, and willing to die trying. I wanted to be a lady King Pin. Which was the equivalent of a CEO of a fortune five hundred company to me. I was determined to prove to every man who'd ever hurt me, and used me that I didn't need any of them for anything.

I moved in an apartment with a Roger's sister Shelly. We had formed somewhat of a friendship after my daughter Monica was born.

We were total opposites. She only dated men with money or "Baller's" which was the term used to describe dope dealers who had big money. Shelly was tall and skinny; high yellow, with long hair, and big breasts. She thought she was the best thing since sliced bread.

She was confident, and conceited. She played the damsel in distress routine better than anyone I'd ever seen, and men ate it up. They showered her with money, gifts and cars. She didn't know how to cook, and refused to clean. She required all of them to wine, and dine her; pay her bills, and take her shopping.

Shelly didn't love anyone or anything as much as she loved herself, and money. All she had to do was spread her legs, and open her hand, and they'd do just about anything she wanted. It was like taking candy from a baby the way she used them.

Love wasn't an issue with Shelly. I think that's why they respected her, because she didn't care about their feelings one way or the other. Shelly tried to convince me to play that role, but that wasn't me.

I was stupid and naïve, and liked the idea of being in love, and having a monogamous relationship. Even though none of the men ever loved me, and all of them cheated. I still wanted to be with one man that I loved.

She tried to set me up on a few blind dates, but that never worked out, because I was too independent, and men didn't find that attractive. I guess I got that way, because I'd always had to do everything for myself.

All the men I knew always needed me, so I didn't know how to depend on a man. Shelly had a man for every night of the week.

While I spent most of my time alone. Almost every man that had come into my life was toxic; like a chronic disease that infected my body, and destroyed my spirit. None of them cared about me or what I had been through.

There were a few men that pretended to be decent, but they had issues too. Once I caught one of them wearing my panties; prancing around in the bathroom mirror!

Then there was the handsome, six figure a year; Civil Engineer who was a sex addict and wanted kinky sex and threesomes. They were worst then the cheaters, and abusers.

I attracted the bad boys; the thugs, the men that had nothing whatsoever to offer me, and treated me like mud under their shoes.

I didn't appeal to a goody toe shoe type of man, and deep inside that's the type of girl I was. When I became, Lacy I made up my mind that I was going to focus on making money, so love was no longer a priority to me anymore.

One Friday night I was standing in my usual spot on the corner next to the alley. It was about midnight; the streets were unusually quiet, and no one was out. That usually happened if the police had raided the dope spot, or if everyone had sold out. I only had a few twenty dollar rocks to sell, and then I was going in for the night.

I was standing near the alley next to some old cars when I saw a car approaching. I always kept my gun in my pocket just in case someone tried to rob me.

One of the usual crack heads got out the car. I recognized him from the neighborhood, he'd brought crack from me before, so I wasn't worried. There was another crack head in the car, but I assumed he was buying the dope for him.

We walked away from the street light, so we wouldn't be spotted. He told me he wanted a twenty dollar rock. I didn't feel threaten by him, because he was a regular, so as soon as I let my guard down, and bent down to get my stash from under the dumpster; I felt someone standing behind me pointing a gun in my back.

I didn't have time to reach for my gun before he had his arms wrapped around me; dragging me towards the car. I tried to scream, but nobody in that neighborhood paid any attention to people screaming; that was common. The two of them threw me in the trunk of the car, and drove off. I offered to give them all my drugs, and what little money I had, but they just ignored me.

They drove around with me in the trunk for about ten minutes. I wasn't going down without a fight. When they opened the trunk I starting swinging, and I scratched one of them in the face.

They pulled me out of the trunk by my hair. One of them punched me in the face, and they both subdued me. They took me into a vacant house, and threw me on the dirty floor in the living room.

They tore my clothes off, and took turns beating, and raping me. They forced me to have oral sex with one; while the other viciously had anal sex with me. They urinated on me, and spit in my face.

This went on until I passed out. I woke up the next morning, and they were gone. They had left me for dead. My body was covered in semen, urine and blood. My blouse was torn and the zipper on my jeans was broken.

I sat there in a state of shock, too scared to move. I found some old rags in the house, and tried to clean myself up. I got some water from a water hose a few houses down to wash my face, and then I started walking home.

Cars rode pass me and nobody offered to help me. I guess they thought I was a crack head by the way I looked. I didn't bother to call the police, because that wasn't the way things were handled in the streets. I was a drug dealer, and I knew they wouldn't care what happened to me.

I made it home, and submerged myself in the bathtub, and soaked for hours. I went to the clinic the next day to get a penicillin shot; just in case they had a disease.

I had a broken nose, and fractured ribs. I never told anyone what happened, because I was too ashamed. I just stayed in the bed for a few weeks; put that memory in my vault, and stored it away just like everything else. I stopped selling drugs on the streets after that, because I was afraid that the next time I wouldn't be so lucky.

A few months later I hooked up with a guy name Smiley. He paid me to pick up and drop off packages from different crack houses. I thought this would be safe, and easy. It didn't pay as much as curb serving, but I made more in one day; then I would make working forty hours on a job.

The first few trips were easy. I'd pick up an envelope, or duffle bag full of money or dope, and drop it off wherever I was instructed too. I was not to open the package; just pick it up, and drop it off which was a piece of cake.

I went to the gas station on Florence and Crenshaw to meet a girlfriend who was going to ride along with me. She was late getting to the spot, and my pager was blowing up because they were waiting for my delivery. I was thirty minutes behind schedule, and I knew Smiley was going to be pissed.

I had to drop off a package to a spot in Watts. When I got there I had this funny feeling in my stomach, the kind you have when you suspect your man is cheating.

I told my friend; who wasn't supposed to be with me to stay in the car. The street was empty, not a soul in sight. I walked to the door, and it looked as though it had been kicked in. The frame, and the knob was broken, and I didn't hear a sound.

I tapped on the door and it slowly started to open by itself. I could smell gun powder. Suddenly something told me to get the hell out of there as fast as I could.

When I got home I found out that there was a home invasion robbery, and that everyone in the house was murdered. If I'd gotten there on time I would have been one of them.

The lifestyle I was living was getting harder, and harder every day. People were robbing and carjacking dope dealers left, and right. I stopped wearing jewelry for fear I'd be robbed or killed for it.

You'd think with this many near death experiences I would have woken up, but I didn't. It was if I had a death wish. I was too stupid to see the signs that God was protecting me from danger, so I kept right on trying to hustle.

I started to get paranoid after what happened in Watts.

I knew I had to do something to get money, so I decided to try to do it the right way, so I got a job at a fast food restaurant. It only paid minimum wage, but that was better than nothing.

I worked two weeks, and when I got my pay check it was only two hundred, and fifty dollars.

I looked at the fruits of my labor in utter shock, and realized I'd made more money in one day selling drugs. I couldn't believe people actually worked two weeks for those crumbs. I was so pissed I quit. At first I thought about robbing the place, but I wasn't a thief, so I went back to what I knew best, and that was the dope game.

I knew I had to figure out a way to master the game, so I wouldn't get caught up in a compromising position again. I had to find someone I could trust, and something I could do to make a lot of money, so I could truly get out of the game.

I was tired of struggling making a dollar here, and there; taking penitentiary chances with my life. I wanted the taste of some real money, something tangible that could help me start a new life.

I wanted to open my own business. I always liked fashion, so I figured if I could get enough money I could open my own boutique. My goal was to make at least a hundred thousand dollars so I could leave this life behind.

I realized after all the hustling I'd done; I really had nothing to show for it. I didn't own a house, my car was a bucket, and I had no money in the bank for a rainy day.

There were no pension plan or 401k in the drug game. I began to realize I was just a low level drug dealer; living day by day making scraps, and willing to die for it. I had to do something different, and I had to do it before it was too late.

Chapter Thirteen

Chasing Love and Money

It was the summer of 1986, and I knew I couldn't sell drugs on the streets anymore, so I started working as a Mule; carrying drugs on airplanes. The job paid well, and wasn't as dangerous as some of the other things I'd done to make money.

My roommate Shelly hooked me up with her boyfriend L.C. He was a baller from Inglewood. He promised to pay me twenty-five hundred dollars each trip; to transport drugs, and money to different states. Our first stop was Denver, Colorado. I'd never been anywhere in my life, so instead of being scared, I was excited.

L.C. wrapped the bricks of pure Peruvian flake Cocaine in foil, and put coffee grinds in it to throw off the dogs. He secured Kilos to my body with duct tape. I was dropped off at the airport by one of his workers, and advised to board the plane alone.

There was always someone watching me just to ensure the product reached its destination without being tampered with. I didn't mind; it felt like I was a character in the movie.

When I reached Denver there would be another worker waiting to drive me to the dope spot. I would drop off the package; go to a hotel, and wait for my money. As odd as it may sound, I felt important.

I'd make two trips a week depending on how fast they'd sell out. It was the same routine every week. The good thing about hanging around drug dealers is that they always ate at first class restaurants; drank the finest alcohol, and smoked the best weed. So I rarely had to buy food or liquor.

Months would go by sometimes before I'd see my kids, but I would always send money, because I thought that would compensate for my absence. I tried to convince myself that what I was doing was for them; to give them a better life, but in reality I was doing it out of lust and greed for the good life.

Denver proved to be very profitable, and the more money we made; the more problems we had with the local drug dealers. We were there six months, and had taken most of their clientele, because our product was pure, and uncut.

They didn't like us selling drugs on their turf, and soon words turned into gun fire, and that meant the police, so we left Denver, and moved on to Nebraska like a traveling circus.

It was the spring of 1987; and my goal was to make enough to open my own business, because I was determined to get out of the drug game. I was tired of taking chances with my life and my freedom, and I knew it was only a matter of time before my luck ran out.

Several of friends had already been killed, and others were locked up for life. I was afraid that I would be next. I agreed to take a shipment to Nebraska, and then I was done. I was going to drop off the package, and make a quick turnaround back to California on the next thing smoking.

When I got there; everyone decided to go out to a club for dinner and drinks, and that's where I saw him. This tall; light skin brother, with sexy hazel eyes, pretty white teeth, and a seductive smile.

He was drop dead gorgeous, and had the body of a Greek God. He stood about six feet six. I couldn't take my eyes off him. I had the waitress send him a drink. That was the first time I'd ever done that, but I had to let him know I was interested.

He walked over to the table to thank me, and introduced himself as Keith. I'd never met anyone as attractive as him before, not even James could hold a candle to him.

He asked if he could sit down, and of course I said yes. We talked until the club closed. I invited him back to my hotel, but he refused which was strange to me. The guys in Los Angeles would jump at the chance, but Keith was different, and that intrigued me.

We exchanged numbers; I told him I was leaving for California the next day, and to come see me before I left, and he agreed. The next morning bright and early to my surprise I heard a knock at the door; it was Keith.

He wouldn't come in the room; instead he waited in the lobby for me to get dressed. He took me to breakfast, and then for a walk in the park. He was such a gentleman; opening doors, and pulling out chairs. Treating me in a way I wasn't use to. He was nothing like any of the thugs I knew.

Keith had manners; was intelligent, and thoughtful. I was determined to pursue him. So I wasn't leaving Nebraska until I did. He dropped me off at my hotel, and promised he'd come back to take me out later that night.

My turn around trip lasted two weeks, and Keith and I spent every waking moment together. I started to believe he was intimidated by me, because he wouldn't touch me, or come in my hotel room.

After a couple of weeks, I'd finally found a way to get him in my room. I told him I slipped in the bathroom, and injured my back. He rushed over to take care of me like the kind person he was, and that night turned into one of the most exciting nights I'd ever had.

We laughed, and talked for a while, then we played dominoes, and cards. Keith didn't drink much, but I lured him to take a drink so he could unwind. I could tell he was inexperienced when it came to sex by the way he looked at me when I talked dirty to him, and that made me feel good because my goal was to turn him out and get him sprung.

I gave him a massage with hot oil, and kissed him from head to toe. I gave him oral sex that made his toes curl, and when he told me he'd never done it before, I decided to teach him. We had passionate freaky sex until the sun came up. It felt good to be in control for once.

I told him all about my life with the exception of having children. I was afraid that he wouldn't want me, so I decided not to share that information.

Keith told me he was twenty-five, and had no kids. I was twenty-four with two. I knew all too well the quickest way to run a man off was to tell him you had a readymade family. My intention was to keep him as my boy toy, and have a little fun.

Keith was oblivious to the drug game. I told him I wanted to get out of that life, and open my own business. Keith was in college with dreams of going to the NBA. He had his life all mapped out, and that was refreshing to me, because I didn't know too many guys with a five year plan.

The time had come for me to go back to California, we said our goodbyes, and I thought that was the end of that. Keith and I had a long distance romance for a couple months. He called me every day to say good morning, and every evening to say good night.

I liked him more than I anticipated, and I flew back and forth a few times to deliver drugs just so I could see him. The day finally arrived when he told me he loved, and missed me. No other man I'd ever been with said those words to me unless I said it to them first, and none of them ever meant it.

Things were moving very fast, and before I knew it four months had passed, and our relationship had gotten pretty serious. In August 1987 we decided to move in together.

We had the perfect relationship, nothing close to what I was accustomed to. I knew it was just a matter of time before he found out about my children from somebody else, and I knew I had to be the one to tell him. I was afraid I would lose him, but much to my surprise he accepted the news fairly well.

I was Raven when I was with Keith, and I was Lacy in the streets. Whenever my entourage was around I had to become Lacy, because that's who they knew, and respected.

One night two guys from my click showed up at our house at midnight unannounced. Keith thought that was disrespectful and asked me to tell them to leave, but that wasn't uncommon to me because you don't work nine to five in the drug game. Sometimes we'd work all night, and sleep all day. That was the nature of the beast.

I was too afraid to expose myself as weak; timid Raven, so rather than remove my mask, I became Lacy and reminded Keith that I paid the bills, and the one who pays the bills makes the rules. To add insult to injury I got dressed, and left with them at one o'clock in the morning without saying a word to Keith.

I disrespected him in the worst way, because I knew he was naïve, and I thought I had him wrapped around my finger.

I was like night and day. When Keith, and I were alone I was Raven the homemaker, but the minute someone else came around I became Lacy the dope dealer.

Whenever L.C. or Shellie would call I'd drop everything. Whatever they asked me to do, I did it; no questions asked. Lacy was true to the game, but not to her man. I cheated on Keith a few times, and I justified it by telling Keith if he didn't like it, he could leave, knowing he had nowhere to go.

Lacy was a real bitch, and had no conscience. Once Shellie had a verbal argument with a chick who lived in Nebraska, and she called me from L.A and told me to handle it, and I did.

I gathered a few people from our crew and we did a drive by. I called the girl to tell her I was coming, and warned her to get the kids out of the house, but she laughed as though it was a joke; so we shot up the house with everyone in it. That's how loyal Lacy was to the streets. I knew what goes around, comes around, and I would reap what I sowed, but I just didn't care.

In November 1987, I found out I was pregnant again with baby number three. It came as a complete shock to me, because several doctors had told me I couldn't have any more children, because of all the damage I'd done to my body having multiple abortions.

My daughters were five and seven at the time, and I really didn't want another child. When I told Keith he was over-joyed and excited, but I was scared and confused. I didn't want another baby out of wed-lock or another baby daddy, so I told Keith I wanted to get an abortion.

He begged me to keep his baby; promising me he would marry me. I knew this baby must be a miracle, because I had unprotected sex numerous times in past relationships and one night stands, and didn't get pregnant, so I decided to keep it.

I was still in the drug game, but I wasn't in as deep as I was before. I was under the impression that I had a real man now; who was going to take care of me, so I wouldn't have to sell drugs anymore.

I wanted a normal life with a man who loved me. I wanted to settle down; get my kids, buy a house with the white picket fence and live happily ever after. I told everyone I was getting out of the game. I can't say they were happy about my decision, but they respected it.

Money was running through my hands like water. Keith didn't make much money working part time, and attending college. It didn't bother me that I had to pay for everything because I knew once Keith got drafted to the NBA he would take care of me and the children.

We lived in an exclusive part of town, in a beautiful townhouse that Keith got in his name because I had no job or credit. Everything we owned was brand new. I didn't use credit cards, because in my mind people who needed credit were poor, so I paid for everything in cash.

We had the best of everything; new cars, furniture, clothing and jewelry. I spoiled Keith because he was good to me, and what little he did have, he didn't have a problem contributing it to our household.

A few months went by, and all the spending had left me nearly broke. I was down to a few thousand dollars. I was now three months pregnant and I really didn't want to sell drugs anymore; especially in that condition.

Keith's income couldn't support our lifestyle, so I decided to get back on the grind. I told Keith I'd make a few more drug runs just long enough for him to get drafted into the NBA.

I truly believed he would make it. I guess I was gullible, and living in a fantasy world because I believed every word Keith said, and never questioned him about anything.

I flew back to California; picked up the bricks of uncut cocaine and hopped on a plane bound for Nebraska. A few days later I got a call from L.C telling me he was sending two new girls down, and they were going to take a cab to the spot, and that he wanted me to pick them up, and bring them to my place until their flight left that night, so I agreed.

When we got to my house Keith was asleep, the girls wanted to shower and take a nap. When they woke up we decided to get dressed, and go out to dinner since they were catching the red eye flight back to California.

I started getting dressed when suddenly I heard a big bang; almost like a bomb, and suddenly my front door came crashing down, and the police stormed in with guns drawn.

They were swinging in through the windows on ropes, and climbing over the balcony, it was like something out of the movie

Scarface.

They had guns pointed at our heads, and told us to get down on the floor.

They dragged Keith from the bed and threw him on the floor with guns pointed to his head. He had no idea what was going on. We were all handcuffed, and one by one we were taken off to jail.

When we got there they separated us; they took the two girls to one room, and left Keith, and I in another. I had already told Keith if this situation ever happened not to say anything, and he didn't say a word.

The room was a square box with dull gray walls, and a concrete floor. There was a table and a few wooden chairs in the middle of the room. We sat there afraid to say a word for fear the room was wire tapped.

Every so often we would talk to each other in code, which was a language only we understood. I paced around the tiny little room to keep warm, and every so often I would stare out the tiny window in the door just to see if anyone was coming, then all of a sudden I saw both of the girls that transported the drugs being escorted out.

I soon started to realize they must have set us up, or snitched to save themselves. A few hours passed when the police came into the room where Keith and I were being held and informed us that we were under arrest and being charged with possession of fire arms and drugs.

I couldn't believe it; I made a point to never keep drugs where I laid my head, so I knew the police must have planted it or one of the girls must have brought drugs into my house.

I knew we were set up. The police found my guns. A pearl handle twenty- five, and a thirty-eight under the bathroom sink. They found a twelve gauge rifle, and an Uzi in the attic. They found triple beam scales, and other drug paraphernalia.

I tried to tell them that Keith had nothing to do with it, but he was charged because the townhouse was in his name. The next day Keith's name was plastered on the front page of the newspaper. Any chance Keith had of making it to the NBA was ruined, and it was all my fault.

We had to obtain a court appointed Attorney's because I was broke. When we went to court we plead not guilty. We went back and forth to court for a few months when my Attorney called and informed me that the case was thrown out of court because the police didn't have a valid search warrant to enter our apartment.

I was happy it was finally over. I tried to think of other ways to make money, I couldn't get a job because I was pregnant and the thought of working for minimum wage sickened me.

A logical person would have stayed as far away from the drug game as possible, but that was the only way I knew how to make money. Keith had lost everything, his job, scholarship, and his dream of going to the NBA went out the window. His family blamed me, which they had every right to, and they pretty much disowned him.

I was heartbroken for Keith, but he knew my lifestyle when he chose to be with me. It wasn't like I put a gun to his head, and forced him to do anything. I tried to rationalize the situation, but any way I looked at it, nothing changed the fact that his life was ruined because of me.

We were dead broke and I was desperate to show Keith that I had his back. I told him I was going to start making drug runs again to support our family. Keith told me that he didn't want the mother of his unborn child in the streets selling drugs, and that it was his turn to take care of me.

I couldn't believe what I was hearing; a man wanted to take care of me? I knew then that he really loved me, and as much as I didn't want him to do it, I had become accustom to living a certain lifestyle so I introduced him to the drug game.

Keith caught on fast, and before I knew it he'd set up an operation that seemed flawless. His entourage consisted of a few of his family members and a couple of his close friends.

My crew didn't mess with me anymore because they knew I was hot; and that the police were watching me, so I introduced Keith to another drug supplier out of Los Angeles. It worked out better because he sold his Kilos at a better price, and he gave it to me on credit based on my reputation in the streets.

In the first month Keith made fifty thousand dollars, and from that point on there was no turning back. Keith was obsessed with money. He watched Scarface everyday like it was a soap opera. He wanted to be Tony Montana.

They say money is the root of all evil, and I started to see another side of Keith that I didn't know existed. The more money he made the worst things between us became. Sometimes he'd stay gone for days at a time and wouldn't call or answer his phone and when he was home he was distant.

Some people can't handle power, and money; Keith was one of them. He became verbally abusive, and it got to a point that everything I said set him off. He became very possessive and refused to let me have any friends. I wasn't allowed to leave the house without his permission.

One day a friend of mine stopped by and Keith happen to come home. He threw her out of the house like she was yesterday's garbage, and forbid me to let anyone else come to the house.

Then the physical abuse started. At first it was an occasional slap in the face, but then it escalated to being punched with a closed fist, choked, and kicked.

If I asked where he'd been he would beat me, so I stopped asking and when I didn't ask he'd beat me for not caring about where he was. I couldn't win for losing.

When I was five months pregnant He broke my nose and dislocated my jaw, because I found out he was cheating and questioned him about it. After he finished beating me, he'd cry and say how much he loved me, and that he knew I was going to leave him.

He would put me in the shower, and try to clean me up. In some cases when the beatings were really brutal he would drop me off at the hospital emergency room entrance, and leave me there. The nurses knew I was being abused and they tried to get me to call the police, but they didn't understand my life.

One nurse slipped me a card to a battered women's shelter in hopes that I would leave the situation, but I couldn't do that, I was too afraid of what Keith would do if he found me.

The more money Keith made the more insane he became. When I made the money, I had the power and I called the shots.

I tried to leave a couple of times, but he wouldn't give me any money and threatened to hurt me if I did. I realized I didn't know him at all. Sometimes he'd be gone for days with his friends and other women and I'd be stuck at home alone. He never bothered to call to see if I was okay, it was as if I didn't exist to him anymore.

I'd finally had enough and decided that I was going to leave him for good. I thought Keith was out of town, so I packed up my suitcases with as much as I could carry and called a cab to pick me up, but before I could get out the door he showed up unexpectedly.

The look in his eyes was that of rage, I knew I was going to die this time, and I was so tired of all the abuse that I didn't even care. I just wanted this life to be over!

Keith stood in front of the door and for a few moments he just glared at me as though I was an intruder, then he said "Where do you think you're going?" I told him I was going back to California, and before I could say another word his hands were wrapped around my throat, I could feel my temples throbbing and my eyes bulging.

I tried to fight back but it was no use, Keith lifted me off the floor and threw me across the room. I laid there for a minute and thought to myself, this time he's going to kill me. Then out of nowhere he calmly said, "If you want to leave then get out."

I didn't move, I just laid there; stiff as a board, because I knew it was a setup and as soon as I moved an inch he would attack me. I just stayed in that same spot while he yelled and screamed and threw things at me.

Just when I thought things couldn't get worse, Keith walked up to me; grabbed me by my hair and drug me across the living room floor. He forced me to stand up and began ripping my clothes off.

He opened the front door and shouted "get out"! I stood there drowning in tears, begging the man I loved, the father of my unborn child to please forgive me, and let me stay, but my pleas were on deaf ears.

He pushed me outside into the freezing cold, and slammed the door. I stood there naked, beating on the door, and pleading with him to let me in.

It was about thirty degrees outside, and there was at least two feet of snow on the ground, I could feel my hands, and feet starting to get numb. I knew if I didn't get help soon my baby, and I would die.

I ran to the nearest neighbor praying someone would answer the door. It was now midnight, and I was sure no one in their right mind would open the door for a black, naked, stranger.

I tried my best to cover myself, but it was no use. I knocked on the door, and rang the doorbell when I heard a women's voice through the door, say "who's there?" I tried to speak but it was so cold I could barely say a word, and then the door opened and there in front of me stood an elderly white couple.

Their eyes grew wide when they saw that I was completely nude, and pregnant. They ushered me inside, and immediately wrapped me in a blanket.

The women introduced herself as Maggie, and her husband as Howard. She made me some hot chocolate, and for few minutes there was nothing said.

Maggie took me into one of the bedrooms, and began going through the closet looking for clothes. She gave me a bra that was two sizes too big, a tee shirt and some sweat pants.

After I showered I sat down with the kind hearted couple and began to tell my story; when I was suddenly interrupted by Maggie; who said "you don't have to stay in an abusive relationship".

She told me that she could hear my scream many times, and that she would always pray for me. She told me that she was in an abusive relationship in the past, and that if I didn't get out it would only get worse.

I told her I was trying to leave when he caught me.

Maggie put her arms around me, and hugged me like my mother would when I was hurt. She told me she would get me a bus ticket home on one condition; that I promised to leave Keith, and never come back.

The next morning Howard and Maggie took me to the bus station. They gave me a brown paper bag with a sandwich, an orange, and a bottle of water in it, along with some pocket change, and sent me on my way. The three day bus ride gave me a chance to rethink my life.

I couldn't understand what happened or how things got to this point; all I knew was my relationship with Keith was over.

I'd come to the conclusion that I tolerated Keith's abuse because I felt responsible for ruining his life. I thought he needed me, and that I could save him.

Every time he hit me; he'd ball up in a corner like a fetus, and cry. He would chant "nobody loves Keith but Keith" over, and over. He used reverse psychology on me, and had me thinking it was my fault, and that I made him hit me.

I knew if I didn't get away from him one of us was going to end up dead, and I didn't want it to be me. The Keith I loved was gone, I had created this monster. I wondered when he looked in the mirror who did he see?

Chapter Fourteen

Willing and Ready to Die

As usual my mother was there to rescue me. She picked me up from the bus station greeting me with open arms. That was one thing I loved about my mother, she never held grudges or said "I told you so".

My father was a different story. Although daddy didn't talk much, when he did say something; you were definitely going to hear the hard core truth.

When we pulled up to the house my daughters were in the front yard playing. They had gotten so big. My oldest was now eight and my baby girl was six. I hadn't seen them in months, and when they saw me they ran up to me, and hugged me so tight it brought tears to my eyes.

I went into labor a few months after I got back to California, on a hot, sunny day in August 1988. My sister Lisa dropped me off at the emergency room, and departed. A few hours later I gave birth to a seven pound, thirteen ounce boy. This time Mama wasn't there; I had to endure this delivery all alone.

I decided to name my beautiful son Michael. He had a head full of silky black hair, and looked just like his father. The doctors said there were complications, and that his lungs hadn't fully developed. He had difficulty breathing, and needed to be hospitalized until he could breathe better on his own.

I guess all the physical; mental and emotional abuse had affected him too. It didn't help that I drank; smoked cigarettes and occasionally dabbled in drugs while I was pregnant. I was so stressed out all the time that I couldn't stop.

To make matters worse I developed diabetes so both of us stayed in the hospital for nearly a month. I really thought things were going to be different this time around, but I was wrong again. I'd made yet another poor choice in a man, and as circumstances dictated my son was fatherless just like the others. A few weeks had come and gone, and somehow Keith found out I had the baby.

He called and asked if he could see his son. I was still hurt and angry because of everything Keith had done to me. I was mad about all the broken promises; the abuse and everything I had sacrificed to love this man only to be lie too, cheated on and mentally and physically tortured. The fact that our relationship was over and I had to deliver our baby alone didn't help either.

I didn't feel Keith deserved the pleasure of seeing our son, but Mama told me no matter what happened between us, I should still allow Keith to be a part of his life. I was reluctant because Keith was not the same man I'd met and fell in love with. He had transformed into someone I didn't want my son to know.

After a few weeks; I finally agreed to let Keith see the baby, but it was going to be on my terms. Keith begged me for weeks to bring the baby to see him, because he had a fear of flying, and like a fool I accommodated him.

When we arrived Keith seemed to be his old self again. He apologized for everything that happened. He said that he was under a lot of stress, and that he never meant to take it out on me.

I could see the drug game had taken a toll on him, he looked worn out, and skinny; not as attractive as I remembered.

He swore he'd changed, and that he wanted to get back together, and be a family, so for the sake of our son, I told Keith I would give him another chance.

A week had gone by when I realized the baby was unable to keep food down, and every time I fed him he'd throw up. His body was limp, and he was non-responsive.

I told Keith, and we rushed him to the emergency room. The doctor examined him, and told us that they thought Michael had spinal meningitis.

I was devastated when the doctor told us they had to give our three month old baby a spinal tap, and that the procedure required them to insert a long needle into his spine.

I couldn't imagine the pain my baby was about to endure. We signed the release forms and sat in the waiting room for several hours waiting for the results.

The test results came back, and confirmed that the test was positive for meningitis. Michael had to remain in the hospital's Intensive Care Unit, and there was nothing I could do to help my little helpless baby. They put needles in his tiny little arms and legs and placed him in a bed with a tent over it.

The doctors didn't know if he was going to live or die; and I was beside myself with fear of losing my baby. Then out of the blue Keith said; "Well lets go, there's nothing we can do for him by staying here" I nearly lost my mind! I told him I wasn't leaving my baby; that if he wanted to leave then he should go. At that moment all the fear I had of Keith was gone.

I realized that the love I had for my son was stronger than anything Keith could say or do to me. Instead of this horrible situation bringing us closer together; it pushed us further apart.

Keith stood there for minute glaring at me as if he wanted to slap the teeth right out of my mouth, and without saying a word; he picked up his jacket, grabbed his keys and left.

I stayed at the hospital for the next several days praying for a miracle. I slept in a recliner next to Michael's bed. I wouldn't even leave to change clothes or eat. The nurses were so kind; they would bring me a tray of food, and clean towels to wash up.

Keith would call occasionally, but he rarely came to see our son. As weeks went by the doctor informed me that Michael was going to be alright, so I started going home for a few hours a day to shower, and sleep.

The day came when the hospital released Michael. I was so overjoyed, I couldn't wait to bring him home. Keith didn't seem to care; he didn't say much and took his time getting dressed to take me to the hospital. Things between Keith and I had been strained ever since he left the hospital the first day Michael was admitted.

We hardly talked to each other at all, because Keith showed little to no interest in our son whatsoever. He never tried to bond with Michael, and after a few weeks of Michael's release from the hospital;

I found out that Keith had another baby just a few months younger then Michael.

When I confronted him; he denied it. I found out who the woman was and where she lived from Keith's sister. When I called her she told me that she had a relationship with Keith that resulted in a child. I went to her house to discover her baby looked just like mine.

Keith refused to claim the child, and even told his mistress that it wasn't his child, and to never talk to me again. I regretted my decision to take Keith back. He was worse than I imagined. He had turned into one of the coldest men I'd ever met, and I was to blame.

I didn't know what to do, I had no money and no means of escape. I didn't want to ask my parents to help me again, so I tried to figure out a way to get some money so I could leave Keith.

It was a quiet Sunday night; I was sitting in the living room rocking the baby to sleep when Keith came home. I could tell he was in one of his moods so I got up to take the baby into the bedroom, when Keith started rambling on and on; saying that I loved the baby more than I loved him, and that I was giving the baby all my attention.

I couldn't believe what I was hearing, I told him the baby needed me because he couldn't do anything for himself, and that he shouldn't feel that way. He was pouting, and complaining as if I was his mother. It was as if I were talking to a spoiled child. I tried my best to convince Keith that I loved him even though I really didn't anymore, but my efforts were in vain.

After an hour of useless arguing; I told Keith I was tired and turned to walk away with the baby in my arms, and without warning I felt something fly past my face, just missing the baby's head, and exploding against the wall. The impact so powerful that it took my breath away, and I fell to my knees and covered the baby with my body.

I looked on the ground and saw the T.V. remote control lying on the floor next to me shattered to pieces. Keith had thrown it at me in anger. I didn't know what to do so I got up and ran into the bedroom in hopes that he wouldn't continue the violence.

Keith came into the room where I'd just laid Michael in his crib and started to yell at me at the top of his lungs; waking up the baby. I reached for Michael to try to calm him down, but Keith grabbed my hands, and told me to let him cry.

I sat there in tears as I watched my frightened baby cry and I could do nothing. I soon realized that Keith was jealous of his own child. In my mind it was only a matter of time before he directed his anger towards him, and I wasn't going to let that happen.

I got up from the bed and went into the living room to try to cool the situation down. I pretended to act as though I understood the way he felt. I reassured him that he meant more to me than anyone else in the world. I hugged, and kissed him, and told him I would cook him a nice dinner.

I prepared Porterhouse steaks; baked potatoes and corn on the cob. I poured us a glass of wine, and we sat down together and ate without saying a word to each other.

When we finished eating; I put on some music and made him a bubble bath. I washed his back, and gave him a massage until he fell asleep.

Once I was sure he was in a deep sleep, I went into the bathroom where he kept the guns hidden under the floor board beneath the vanity. I found the forty-five caliber automatic, and I knew I had to kill him; if I wanted to get me, and my baby out alive.

I walked into the room; stood over the bed and pointed the gun at his head. I pulled the trigger, but nothing happened.

I continue to try to shoot when I discovered the clip wasn't in the gun! Keith woke up to see me standing over him pointing a gun at his head.

I kept pulling the trigger over and over frantically trying to force a bullet out of the gun, while Keith lay there watching in tears.

I was willing to kill or die for my son! He was an innocent baby; and it was my job to protect him from anyone who would try to hurt him including his own father.

I wanted so badly for Keith to a least love him. I prayed that things would be different. I wanted our life to be perfect the way I'd always imagined, but I couldn't subject my baby to any harm.

Keith knew I had snapped, and he was lucky to be alive. The next day he let me leave without a fight. I packed my bags; called a cab and took my baby back to California for good.

Chapter Fifteen

Justice and Mercy

Life for me was never easy. It seemed no matter where I turned, bad things were waiting for me just around the corner. It was February nineteen-eighty-nine, and I moved back to California without Keith. I got a job, and an apartment and I was surviving on my own.

I was determined to turn my life around. Finally I could see the light at the end of the tunnel, and it felt good to be able to breath without fear of being beaten for breathing too loud.

It had been months since I left Keith, and I was in a good place mentally, and emotionally. I once believed I couldn't make it without a man, but I had proven myself wrong, and was doing a great job at reinventing myself. I didn't have much, but the sense of security I developed made me feel like I had plenty.

It was a Monday morning, and I was on my way to drop Michael off to daycare, when the phone rang. I recognized the Nebraska area code, and immediately thought it was Keith calling from a different number.

I'd been avoiding him for months, but he was tenacious, and no matter how many times I changed my number he always managed to get it. I started to think it was an inside job, and that he was paying one of my sisters or my brother to give to give him my number.

I was reluctant to answer at first, so I let it ring several times before picking it up. The voice on the other end of the line was that of an older Caucasian man.

He introduced himself as Detective Tom Downing from the Drug Taskforce unit in Omaha, Nebraska. I didn't say a word for a few seconds because I was speechless. He went on to tell me that Keith and I had been under surveillance for over a year, and that there were going to be warrants issued for our arrest.

At first I thought this must be some kind of joke, and that Keith had paid someone to call me just to scare me. So I laughed; told him to go screw himself, and hung up the phone.

When I spoke to Keith he insisted that he had nothing to do with it and told me it wasn't a joke. He told me that we needed to meet in person so we could talk, and when he got the courage to fly out to California I knew it was something serious.

The next day I received a call from my friend Penney. We had transported drugs together numerous times. She told me she saw mug shots of Keith, and me on the news, and that they said we were armed and dangerous!

I ran to turn the television on, but by the time I found the channel it was off. I didn't know what to do, so I dropped the phone and ran out the house in sheer panic.

I called Keith from a pay phone, and told him the news. I picked up Michael, and hid in a motel for a few days, because I was too scared the police would raid my house.

Keith and I had done a lot of dirt in the streets, and we made a lot of enemies. I thought because I got out of the drug game I was in the clear, but I guess I was wrong.

Keith, and I hooked up in San Francisco a week later. He told me that several people in Nebraska had been arrested in drug raids, and that everyone was snitching to avoid going to prison.

He said we needed to get married as soon as possible so that if we got arrested; we wouldn't be forced to testify against each other.

In the beginning of our relationship I dreamed of marrying Keith because I thought he was a good man, but when he turned into this cold-hearted, notorious drug dealer; I knew that would never happen.

The crazy thing about the whole situation was that I still loved him, and I would gladly marry him, but all he wanted was a security blanket not a wife.

He reassured me this was the only way I could avoid prison and that if I didn't do it he'd be forced to testify against me if it went to trial. So we marched down to a little wedding chapel with our son, and got married the next day. We didn't even consummate the marriage.

Keith drove me to the bus station, and we said our goodbyes. He stayed in Northern California, and continued to do his thing, but I could feel it was only a matter of time before it all came crashing down. Three days later Keith got arrested.

When I found out there was a warrant for my arrest I was ready to run. I told my parents the news, and was preparing to take my kids, and flee to Mexico.

My father sat me down, and bluntly said; "you can't keep running from everything, you have to grow up, and face what you've done". I knew he was right, and a few days later I called the FBI, and informed them that I wanted to turn myself in.

My mother kept my children while my father drove me down to the federal building on Wilshire Blvd in Los Angeles. Daddy was never one to show emotion, but when we got there, and the Federal Marshalls handcuffed me, I looked at my father, and there were tears in his eyes.

He asked them why they had to put handcuffs on me, and they advised him it was their procedure. That was the first time in my life my father said the words "I love you" to me; as the Federal Marshalls took me away.

I was held in the Metropolitan Detention Center for several months until I was extradited back to Nebraska to stand trial. I was charged with seventeen counts of Conspiracy. Drug trafficking; money laundering, tax evasion, and distribution of a controlled substance, this list was endless.

There were so many charges against me that they started to sound the same. I was even charged with selling drugs to minors near a school which was double penalty if convicted.

The truth of the matter is I'd never sold drug to children, because, I had kids of my own, and would never want someone to give them drugs.

There were forty-five people listed in the indictment and Keith, and I were at the top of the list. The Federal Marshalls had captured everyone listed in the indictment prior to me turning myself in.

They were able to catch Michael because he called someone in Nebraska from his cell phone, and their phone was tapped.

By the time I got to court everyone had already snitched, and I was left holding the bag. I was the "so-called" Leader and Organizer of the drug ring.

My Attorney informed me that I was facing twenty-five years to life in prison, and that the only thing that would save me was if I plea bargained, and testified against Keith,

As much as Keith had cheated, used and abused me I still couldn't let my husband and the father of my son spend his life in prison.

I realized this situation was bigger than me, but I had my family to think about, and I didn't want to put them in danger.

I called mama, and asked her to pray for me. I always felt God was unhappy with the decisions I'd made, but my mothers' prayers always seemed to get answered.

In my eyes she had a special connection with God. Her faith gave me hope. I told my Attorney I wouldn't testify against Keith. I just had to face the music, and see what happens.

She asked me why I loved and trusted him so much. Then she told me "off the record" that Keith gave me up, he used me as a scape goat, and didn't think twice about it, and that's why I was named the leader and organizer.

She thought I was crazy, but based on my mothers' faith that God would deliver me I refused to give him up. I knew I had done wrong in the past, but I didn't think I'd done anything to deserve life in prison.

I always believed you reap what you sow, and even though I had gotten out of the game, and tried to turn my life around; my past came back to haunt me.

Mama told me she'd gone on a seven day fast, and that God told her that I would have to go to prison for what I'd done, but that I wouldn't get life.

Once I heard that, I was at peace. The trial lasted for six months, there were thousands of wire taps tapes submitted into evidence but the Feds couldn't find anything I said to incriminate myself.

There were surveillance photos taken, but I was not in any of those. There were drugs confiscated at the airport, and the crack houses raided, and there was no evidence whatsoever that I knew anything about it.

Everything they had against me was based on hearsay and snitches; who were trying to save themselves and obtain a get out of jail free card.

As I sat in the courtroom alone; awaiting my fate, the judge asked me to stand to my feet. He looked at me with a look of utter disgust as he described me as a "failure to society". He told me I destroyed many lives that could never be repaired, and as I listened to the things the judge said about me, deep inside I knew I wasn't the person the judge described.

I stood there with tears running down my face, not for fear of what I was facing, but for fear of what I had become. My parents didn't raise me like this, I didn't have to do any of the things I'd done. I had a choice and I chose the wrong path.

I had disappointed God, my parents, and my children, but for some unknown reason God let them find favor with me and before the judge sentenced me, he told me I should thank the prosecutor for their recommendation because if it was left up to him I would get the maximum sentence the law allowed.

The Federal Prosecutor offered to reduce my charges to three counts of conspiracy if I plead guilty. My mother was right, God had mercy on me. It was nothing short of a miracle. I was convicted of drug conspiracy and sentenced to thirty-eight months in prison in December nineteen-ninety.

The judge was even kind enough to allow me time to turn myself in so that I could spend some time with my children and get my affairs in order. I was thankful for that. I had gotten closer to my two beautiful daughters, and realized just how much of their life I had missed out on.

March 1991 on a gloomy spring day I turned myself in. I'd never been more scared in my life; then I was that day. I'd never been in any real trouble before; except for the time my cousin Patricia, and I spent a few days in county jail over a prank we pulled in Santa Monica.

It was a Friday night, and we decided to go out to Santa Monica and cruise the boulevard. We were both pregnant at the time I was a five months and Patricia was three. We had our boyfriends with us, and two friends.

We were walking down Melrose with our friend Tink determined to find him a boyfriend. What we didn't know was while we were walking ahead the other guy that came along with them had robbed some of the male prostitutes.

We heard screaming in the distance, and they told us to run so we ran without knowing why we were running. Before we knew what was happening the police swarmed in and arrested all of us, and took us to jail.

They held Patricia, me and our boyfriends for three days and they sent Tink to juvenile hall because he was a minor. They charged the other guy with theft, and kept him in jail. That was nothing compared to what I was facing now; this was the real thing.

I was handcuffed, and shackles were placed around my ankles. It was difficult to walk, and every time I took a step the shackles would tighten and hurt my ankles. All I could do was take short steps to keep from falling.

We were then placed on a federal airplane just for prisoners. There were armed Marshalls on board with sub machine guns. We were not allowed to talk to each other or even have eye contact. The plane made several stops dropping inmates off and picking inmates up. I spent months in Oklahoma in a holding facility for federal inmates. It was a nightmare.

I was forced to strip naked in front of officers, and other inmates. I had to bend over, spread my butt cheeks, and cough. That was the first time anyone had ever seen me totally nude. The embarrassment, and disgrace I endured was indescribable. I felt belittled and degraded as they stared and yelled obscenities at me. To make matters worse, I was required to wear this hideous orange jumpsuit with the prisons name plastered on the back of it and plastic flip flops. This was the price I had pay for committing a crime.

I was put into a tiny cell alone that had nothing but a metal bed with a thin plastic mattress about an inch thick. They gave me one flat pillow, and an itchy wool blanket. There was a toilet and a sink with a small plastic mirror that was distorted so when you looked in it you looked like someone in a circus fun house, but nothing about this was fun.

All I did was think; day in and day out. I couldn't shut down my brain or stop the visions in my head from playing like a movie in my mind. It was as if I was being haunted with my past, present and future at the same time.

For years I tried to hid my skeletons and erase my demons with drugs and alcohol. I was sober now; there was nothing to alter my thought process, nothing to help me forget all the bad decisions and poor choices I'd made. I came face to face with reality and that's when my life became real.

The first few days were the hardest; it was like I was a junkie coming down off of heroin. Some days I would just cry, some nights I would just scream, and other times I would do a thousand jumping jacks and sing all the old gospel hymns I remembered from church.

I would talk out loud to God; tell him how sorry I was for doing all the horrible things that I'd done. I told him how ashamed I was of myself, because I knew right from wrong. I was practically raised in church, there was no excuse for my behavior.

I didn't ask God for forgiveness, because I didn't think I deserved it. Mama always told me to call on the one I served; that crossed my mind over and over, because I knew the one I served wouldn't help me; because the one I served is the reason I was here.

I had given my entire life to the devil, and when I got in trouble the only one I called on was God. How ironic? Instead I thanked God for his mercy, I for sparing my life. I'd been given a second chance at life, and I knew I had to do something good with it.

When I finally reached what would be my place of residence for the next few years; a fear came over me that I could not explain. I couldn't run anymore, I had to face the truth. I spent a lot of time thinking about all the things I'd done to my children and my family; all the people I'd hurt, and the lives I destroyed. I was selfish and self-centered. I thought of no one else but myself all my life.

Most of my life was make-believe; even in the drug game I put on a front, because I couldn't let anyone know that I wasn't what I proclaimed to be. I wasn't this hard core drug dealer without a conscience.

The picture I painted of myself couldn't be further from the truth. I believed in God; I prayed, and I had remorse for everything I'd done. I knew the lifestyle I was living wasn't who I really was or what I really wanted to do, but I did it anyway just fit it. I wanted attention and respect, and I did whatever I had to do to get it.

Federal prison was nothing like I expected. It looked like a college. There were three buildings with separate wings; unit A-B, C-D and E-F. I was appointed to unit C-D.

I was expecting bar doors and dirty concrete floors. Instead there were private doors on each room with a little window in the front and knobs which required a key to get in. Turns out I'd lucked up and got assigned to the unit built for Patty Hurst by her father when she was in prison.

There was carpet throughout the common areas. There was a kitchen, professional beauty salon, two TV rooms, and private showers with doors.

There were four bunk beds in the room I was in. They considered that the holding cell. That's where everyone resided until they were assigned to a two person room.

A majority of the women like myself were locked up because of a man; either helping him or having to hustle herself to feed her children, because there was no father in the picture.

Most of the women had children they'd left behind to be raised by their grandmother's or other family members. I was one of them, and I'd made up my mind this time that I was going to change, because I didn't want to return home to the same life I'd left behind.

I enrolled in school, and got my GED. I realized that walking across my high school stage with an empty diploma case was all for show. I was short two credits the last semester of high school, and the counselor failed to inform me until it was too late. It took me going to prison to finally do something about it.

At first I had a hard time taking orders from the guards. I guess I got that way because of every man I'd ever been with barking commands at me as if I was a dog. When I got to prison it was hard for me to adapt to the rules.

Every inmate was required to work. I didn't have a problem with that, because I figured it would make the time go by faster if I kept busy.

Things didn't start out good, because I was forced to work in the kitchen; washing dishes, and mopping floors and that didn't work well for me, and when I refused to do it I found myself in "the hole" a term used to describe solitary confinement.

I was there for thirty days, but to me it was better the being the white man's "house nigga". When I was released I got a job as a plumber. It paid twenty-five cents an hour. When they told me, I wanted to quit but that would mean more time in the hole so I decided to make the best of it, and that's just what I did. I remembered quitting jobs in the free world that paid a whole lot more, now I was reduced to working for change.

I was always good with my hands so I thought I would benefit from being a plumber and besides if I mastered the skill I could do that in the free world because plumbers made a lot of money.

It had its advantages as well. I got to go to the men's camp to work sometimes, and I had access to tools, which would prove to come in handy. I didn't have any money left when I went to prison; the feds had taken everything we had.

My parents could hardly afford to send me anything, and I didn't expect them to, because they had my three children to take care of.

I knew I had to do something to make money, and since I was an alcoholic it was only logical for me to kill two birds with one stone; sell what I love and love what I sell! So I became skilled at making "Hooch" which is a form of liquor made with yeast, oranges, lemons, and grapefruit.

It had a taste similar to vodka, but was twice as potent. The key to making good hooch was to place it in a warm area, and let it sit for at least three days, and since I was a plumber with access to tools; I hid it in the vents.

I knew that was a clever idea, and the last place anyone would think to look. Whenever the officers did have a shakedown they would never find it. I sold it for twenty dollars a cup, and I was making a killing.

I had a cool operation in place. My roommate Kelsey worked in the kitchen, so she'd steal everything I needed including the empty gallon milk jugs. I'd pay her in commissary once a week. Each gallon would make roughly ten cups, I would make two jugs at a time at least three times a week.

We stayed drunk, and I stayed getting paid. Some of the inmates would pay me by having their family put money on my books, and others would pay with commissary. This proved to be a lucrative money making scheme until I pissed somebody off.

Like the streets; there's always a snitch to tell if they don't get what they want. Before I knew it; the alarms went off which meant there was going to be a shake down. When this occurred we were to stay put until they released us to our unit.

I was at work when the alarm sounded, my boss looked at me; laughed, and said "What did you do now?" I was known for getting in trouble, and I tried to laugh it off, but I was worried that they'd found my stash.

I saw the guards running towards my unit with dogs, and I knew it was about to go down. I could hear a voice on my sergeants' two way radio saying that the dog found something so strong that it rendered the dog unconscious. They had to carry the poor dog out of the unit on a stretcher.

After thirty minutes they released me to go back to my unit. I walked across the campus at a snail's pace, and my heart was racing.

When I walked into my dorm, I noticed that all the other doors were open, and the inmates were standing next to their beds. My door was shut, and my roommate was standing outside trying to unlock it.

As soon as I reached the door, we were surrounded by guards. They told us to get against the wall, and we were both handcuffed and taken to the Hole.

I was locked up for sixty days this time. They released my roommate after I told them she had nothing to do with it. I made a lot of friends in prison; inmates and guards alike, but I also had a lot of enemies too.

After I was released from the hole the second time, I was warned that if I continued to get in trouble I would be transferred to another facility outside of California; which would make it impossible for me to see my family.

I had only seen my children once. I knew how much of a hardship is was for my parents to come see me. My father was the sole breadwinner and he didn't make much money, but somehow they found a way.

They had my three children, my siblings and their kids living in the household. There were ten people living in a three bedroom house. I knew they were doing the best they could, so I didn't want them to worry about sending me money or trying to visit.

I did what I needed to do to survive, and when I wasn't boot-legging hooch, or selling cough syrup; that I got from the infirmary; I was the unit hair stylist, and barber. I charged five dollars to wash, press, and curl, and three dollars to cut, and trim.

I was a jack of all trades, and I did what I had to do to make a buck. I hooked up with a guard name Samson, he was a tall, nerdy looking Jamaican. I knew Samson had a crush on me, so I used that to my advantage.

I won his trust, and eventually convinced him to sneak in hair weave; dye, liquor, and anything else people wanted, and I charged triple the price. I was a natural born hustler.

I had my share of rivals; most of them were threatened by my straight forward approach, and the fact that I didn't filter my words. There was so much tension between the women from the east coast, and the west coast. It was just like the Crips, and the Bloods.

I had my share of arguments, and disagreements; most of them were because women were envious of my relationship with their "Stud" girlfriends or just plain haters.

One day I was walking from class with a stud named Linda. We were talking about an assignment we were working on together. I didn't know at the time that she was hitting on me; she walked me to my room, and a few hours later there was a knock at my door.

At the time I didn't have a roommate, so I was lying in bed reading a book with nothing but a tee shirt and panties on. I looked through the window, and saw a straggly looking white girl with bad acne standing at my door.

I'd never seen her before, so I opened the door; thinking she might be my new roommate. There were two chubby brunettes' women standing on each side of her like bodyguards.

I asked them what they wanted, and the blonde responded; "if you don't want no problems, you better stay away from Linda." Before I knew what hit me my alter ego Lacy reared her ugly little head and said; "I don't respond well to threats" and slammed the door in her face.

I put on my kakis, and my boots, and went on a mission to find Linda. When I got to her room I told her what happened. She told me she would handle it, but that wasn't good enough for me.

I wasn't having no pink dike come to my room; get in my face, and threaten me. I always referred to white people as pink because in reality they were pink. If I accepted that; then I would be labeled a punk, and everyone would think they could disrespect me.

A couple of days passed; the word traveled throughout the unit that there was going to be a fight. I had to look over my shoulder, and watch my back everywhere I went, because I didn't know when they would try to jump me.

It was a Friday morning. I had to get up at 5 am for work. I grabbed my hygiene products, and my towel, and went to the shower.

I checked out some curling irons from the officer's station, and put them in my robe pocket. I was standing in the hallway ironing my work clothes on the built-in ironing board that was bolted to the wall; when suddenly out of nowhere the straggly blonde who reminded me of the bride of Chuckie walked up to me waving her hands in the air in a threatening manner.

She was yelling, and cursing, and before I knew it we were fighting. I threw her on the ground, and began punching her in her face. I straddled myself on top of her, and began slamming her head against the floor when her friends jumped in. They were pulling my hair; hitting me in my head, and kicking me.

I knew I was out numbered, and they were getting the best of me when some of the women from the West Coast came to my rescue, and we were all fighting.

I didn't know any of the females that were helping me, but there was an unspoken loyalty between us. When they pulled the girls off me; I reached for the curlers that were in my robe pocket, and started swinging. I hit the blonde in the head with the medal curling iron until I saw blood.

Then the alarms sounded, and we all disbursed in opposite directions. I headed for the barber shop along with one of the women who'd helped me in the fight, because it was the closest room I could get to without being seen by the officers.

When we got there she introduced herself as Shanae; and sat down in the barber chair while I pretended to be curling her hair.

The officer asked us what happened, and we adamantly denied knowing anything. I knew he wasn't buying it when he pointed out the blood on my robe. I was handcuffed, and taken to the hole again. This time they were threatening to charge me with assault with a deadly weapon. I found out later that the white girl named Mandy admitted that they'd jumped me, and that I was just defending myself.

I stayed in the hole for three months this time. Shanae and some of the other girls who helped me fight that day would sneak to the back window, and talk to me.

We soon became good friends, and when I was released everyone was waiting outside to welcome me back; even the white girl that I'd beat up waited in line to shake my hand.

There was a level of respect that you earned when you stood your ground, and I'd earned it. I didn't have any more problems out of them or anyone else for that matter.

Believe it or not Federal Prison wasn't that bad. We had a movie theater, skating ring, racquetball, and tennis court. We even had a baseball diamond and teams from the free world would come in every Sunday and play against us.

We had barbeques at least once a month. We ate good food like, steaks, ribs and of course chicken. We had photographer's that came in on the weekend to take pictures of us to send home to our families.

We got to wear our own clothes, shoes and jewelry. As far as

Prisons are concerned, if you had to be locked up that was the place to go. I called it "Club Fed" because compared to state prison it was like a vacation; only you couldn't leave when you wanted too, and there were armed guards instead of waiters and bob wire fences instead of secluded islands.

We all had our share of good days and bad, but the hardest times was when someone died. They'd summon us over the loud speaker to report to the Chaplin. Most of the women couldn't afford to pay the cost of a flight and arm guards so they couldn't attend the funeral, and just had to grieve in their tiny eight by ten cell.

Visiting times and Mail call was extremely difficult for me. Some inmates got mail every day; money on their books and visits every weekend.

I rarely got any letters or money, and I only had one visit the entire time I was locked up. All those "friends" who I'd been down for, and who claimed they loved me; didn't bother to write or visit. It was hard to sit by, and watch as some inmates had weekly visits, money on their books and as many packages as they could buy.

I got involved with the Samson so that I wouldn't lack for anything. He put money on my books and brought me packages with designer clothes, shoes and jewelry in it.

I was on the grind all the time. I hustled; had a girlfriend, and a guard. I made sure to cover all bases, because that's what I knew how to do best.

Ever since I could remember I was confused about my sexuality. I became that way after I was molested as a young child. My pastor would preach about homosexuals going to hell, and say that it was an abomination for two people of the same sex to be together.

I battled with those feelings most of my life. I liked to look at beautiful women, and I didn't think it was as bad as two hairy men laying up humping on each other having anal sex. The idea of that disgusted me.

I never had an orgasm with a man. I didn't know what it felt like to really enjoy sex. I didn't get that warm tingling feeling down there when I was with a man. Prison was the one place I could openly be with a woman, and not be judged.

Most women came in saying they'd never be with a women, but loneliness can make you do things you never expected, and for most of them they ultimately gave in after a while.

I met many different women from all walks of life, and I realized age and race didn't matter because prison didn't discriminate.

There were women bank robbers, drug dealers, computer hackers and embezzlers. If there was one thing prison taught me; it was that there were a lot of women who felt desperate enough to do whatever they had to do to survive?

Many thought they had no other option other than to risk their freedom. Most of them like myself had been in abusive relationships; were single mothers, and suffered from low self-esteem.

I was amazed to meet so many women who had been sexually molested as a child or who were abandoned by their man, and left to raise children on their own.

I was blessed, because I had my mother and father. They were the best grandparents in the world to my children. They loved them probably more than they loved me, and I was all right with that.

When I got out the hole I moved into a room with Shanae. She was brown skinned with long thick black hair, and dark brown eyes. She had dimples in both cheeks, and an infectious smile. The thing I loved the most about Shanae was her outlook on life.

Although she was sentenced to twenty-five years for drug conspiracy; she still maintained a positive attitude. We'd hit it off when she helped me in the fight, and we had a lot in common.

She was from South Central L.A. too. She had a sense of humor out of this world, and no matter how bad a situation was she always found a way to make me laugh.

Shanae only had one child, and he was being raised by her family. Shanae was the rational one between the two of us, so she would try keep me out of trouble as much as she could.

We would sit up all night talking about our lives; our goals, and our dreams. We had a sister bond, and that meant the world to me.

We shared everything unlike me and my real sisters. We were the two most popular; well-known inmates in the entire prison. Shanae was known for her funny demeanor; while I was known for my smart mouth and quick temper. All the captains and officers liked us, and though I got in trouble a few times they still could see right through me, and they knew that I wasn't a bad person.

As time passed I met a girl from the valley name "Alexis". She was just a baby when she arrived to prison for credit card fraud. I took her under my wing, and became her big sister since I was ten years older than her.

Alexis was beautiful, with caramel colored skin, big brown eyes, and dimples. Her hair went down her back, and she had legs that never seemed to end.

 I knew she was going to have trouble, because there were a lot of jealous females in prison. Alexis wasn't in the same unit as Shanae and I, but since I was a plumber I would visit her all the time.

Alexis was nothing like me; she was quiet, and stayed mostly to herself. I think she was intimidated by her surroundings, and that was understandable since she'd lived a sheltered life in an upscale part of town with nannies, and maids.

Alexis was use to nice things, she'd traveled the world as a model, and went to Africa when she was only fourteen. I liked her because she seemed honest, and down to earth.

Most of the girls didn't like her because they thought she was fake, but that was really who she was. Shanae got close to her too, and we quickly became inseparable.

We became three the hard way, and you couldn't say or do anything to one of us without dealing with all of us.

Alexis gave birth to her first child in prison. They let her spend just one day with her baby; then they gave the baby to her mother, and sent her back to prison.

I could only imagine how hard that was for Alexis having her first child in prison, and then only having one day to bond with her. I know it made her sad not being able to see or hold her newborn baby, but like everything in prison you just had to grin and bear it.

There were several other women that I'd gotten very close to, and grew to love. We all had a story, and we were all equal in our pain. Nobody was better than anyone else. We had our occasional disagreements, but for the most part we all got along the best way we could living in a confined space.

We all shared a mutual connection, and that was; we were all women, and we were all convicted felons. We all helped each other get through some really rough times, and they all became my sisters.

Prison was a revolving door for some, but when one would come, another would leave; that was the hard part. Once you got close to someone they would either get released, or get transferred to another prison.

My time had come to finally go home, and I couldn't believe just how much it hurt me to leave my friends behind. I cried for days before I was released, because these women knew me, the real me, and they accepted me with all my flaws, and weaknesses.

There were the few that judged me and didn't like me, but for the most part my real friends really cared about me.

It was hardest to leave Shanae, she was my rock, and even though she was sentenced to twenty-five years she never let it defeat her. She never cried, or complained, and that's why I loved, and respected her so much.

We shared our innermost secrets; the things that hurt us the most, and I felt safe for once in my life because I didn't have to pretend, and that meant everything to me. She accepted me the way I was, and that was something no one else had ever done before.

The night before I was released the girls gave me a going away party, they cooked and we played games, and laughed and cried together until it was lights off.

The next morning, bright and early I heard a knock at my door, it was the guard telling me to get ready, it was time to go. Shanae was in the bunk bed on top of me. I got up slowly and sat on the side of the bed, she sat up in her bed, and we didn't say a word.

We just looked at each other, and I put on my clothes and headed for the door. I picked up my bag and clasped the knob when Shanae said "and you better not come back".

We both laughed, then I told her I would never be back, I opened the door and didn't look back. I cried all the way to the airport. As much as I wanted my freedom, I felt free in prison as crazy as that might seem.

I was released to a halfway house in the Rubidoux, California. I had to remain there for six months before I could go home. I was excited, and couldn't wait to be in the free world again. The halfway house was unisex, so there were male and female convicted felons living there.

We were given chores each week, and we could only leave to search for jobs. I was the only black female in the house. The coordinator and most of the staff were Mexican. I knew they were going to be bias, because that's just the way it was for black people.

I tried to keep my mouth shut, and make the best of it. We had to get up every morning at five am and clean up the room we shared, and do our designated chores.

The first week I was given kitchen detail. I always had a problem with cleaning and mopping up after other people. I did it anyway because I was so close to being free, and I didn't want to jeopardize going back to prison, so I didn't complain.

The next week the little fat Mexican coordinator gave me kitchen detail again. The other Mexican inmates were given light duty. I didn't think it was fair so I addressed the staff with my grievances.

I knew the coordinator didn't like me the first week I arrived, because a few male friends took me shopping and bought me designer clothing and shoes. She tried to make me send them home; stating that I had violated the limit, but when she couldn't show me in writing, she was forced to let me keep them, and she got mad.

I expressed my concerns to her about getting kitchen detail two weeks in a row and she said "do it, or I'll violate you I don't know why I didn't just comply with her demands, I just didn't. Instead I told her where to she could stick that mop; and walked away.

I went to my room and started packing because I knew it was just a matter of time before the Federal Marshalls came to pick me up.

The next morning they were there bright and early. I was violated for disobeying a direct order and immediately sent back to federal prison where I had to complete the remainder of my sentence.

I wasn't out two weeks, and I knew Shanae was going to be angry at me for coming back. Although everyone thought I was crazy, they welcomed me back with open arms.

The day I was released I was dropped off at the Oakland Airport, but I didn't go home. Samson came to pick me up so we could spend some time together before I went home to my family.

He greeted me with a big teddy bear, flowers and balloons. We had gotten very serious over the last two years, and I liked him so much that I quit smoking cigarettes cold turkey just to prove my love for him.

We made plans to be together when I got out, but I had to get my children first. Samson didn't have any kids and he was the first man I'd met that didn't have a problem with me having them. That's what I loved about him the most.

Samson didn't live far from the airport, it was about a fifteen minute drive. When we pulled up to his modest house he jumped out the car and opened my door. He grabbed my hand and led me to the front door. When he opened the door the vision before me was like a dream.

There were rose petals sprinkled on the floor, and candles lit all over the room. There were vases of red roses and a table with beautiful linen and china. I had never been treated this way before. I stood there in tears; I was astounded by how much work he'd done to please me.

Samson gently took my hand and led me into the bathroom, there was a soft white robe and fluffy slippers lying on a chair, he started the bath water, and slowly tried to undress me.

I had never let any man see me completely naked, so I quickly put a halt on that and pretended to be shy. He lit candles and turned off the lights in the bathroom. He brought me a glass of real wine, something I hadn't had in years.

I sank into the tub full of bubbles, and I was in heaven. He put on some jazz and he came into the bathroom, sat on the floor next to me and washed my hair with so much love and tenderness that I could do nothing but relish the moment. I had never met a man like him before, If this was a dream, I never wanted to wake up.

We stayed locked away at his house for three days. We talked about our dreams, and ambitions and we made a promise to be together forever. He helped me make a resume, which is something I'd never done before. I had nothing to put on it so we got creative and made things up.

Samson was very smart, he'd graduated from Berkeley and obtained his master's degree in political science. I couldn't imagine why he wanted a woman like me when he could have any woman he wanted.

Samson told me that he was shy until he met me and that I gave him confidence. He said he feel in love with me because I was real!

If he only knew it was all a liar. I was as fake as a three dollar bill, and that most of my life I lived in a pretend world, he would have took off at full speed and never looked back.

That day I made up my mind that I was going to be all that he wanted and needed in a women. I was not going to disappoint him or my children ever again.

Samson drove me to the airport that Sunday, and I promised him I would be back for good real soon. We said our goodbyes, and I boarded the plane destined to face what I'd left behind.

It's been over twenty years since I left prison, but the bond I built with those strong, courageous woman still remains, and I am still friends with most of them until this very day.

Chapter Sixteen

Never Make a Promise to God

It was now January 1994 it was a sentimental time in my life. I was just released from prison and I realized time was something I could never get back. At age thirty-two I didn't know how to begin living a normal life with a felony and no real job skills.

My daughters were now teenagers, and my son was in the first grade. He was just a baby when I left him. I knew I owed them an explanation about where I'd been for most of their life.

Keith was released from prison a year prior, and Mama being the kind women that she was; let him move in their tiny three bedroom house so that at least one of the kids would have their father around.

Keith never wrote me; put money on my books, or came to visit. He left me in prison for dead and forgot I existed

He stayed with my family for several months until Mama had to kick him out because she found out he had other women calling, and coming to her house to pick him up.

He moved in with some older woman he'd met, and started a new life for himself; taking our son with him. I was glad he didn't leave him behind like my daughter's father had all their life, but I didn't want them separated from each other either. It was a bitter pill to swallow.

I didn't know what I was going to do; all I knew was I had to get my baby back. I'd never really gotten a chance to know my children, like a real mother should, and that was one of my biggest regrets.

At first it was hard, because my daughters really didn't know or trust me. We were like strangers towards each other. It took a while for them to warm up to me especially my oldest daughter Mya. Every time they would call for Mama I would answer, but then I realized they were calling for my mother.

I didn't know what to say to them, or how to explain who I was; and where I'd been for most of their lives. So I just tried to be their friend. I did whatever they wanted me to do just to make them happy.

I didn't have anything when I came home from prison; no car, money or clothes. There was no retirement or pension in the drug game. You either put your money in a Swiss bank account or buried it in the backyard, and I had done neither of the two. I refused to get on welfare again, but I knew I had to do something.

When I found out Keith had a good job, a new BMW, and was living in a big house with his new girlfriend I was pissed. After all the sacrifices I'd made for him; he just moved on like nothing I did mattered.

I begged him to let me see our son, and finally he agreed to meet me at McDonald's. Michael was so cute with his dark brown eyes, long eyelashes and curly black hair. He looked just like Keith, but with my eyes.

At first he wouldn't let me touch him, so I went outside the McDonald's play house and started playing with the other kids, and soon he warmed up to me and let me hug, and kiss him.

I probed to see if he knew who I was; he gave me this puzzled look and said, "You're my Mama", and that was it. I was determined to get him at any cost.

Keith would only let me see him at the McDonald's on Sundays for a while, and I knew the only way I was going to get him back was if I had a job and somewhere stable to live, so I went along with this arrangement.

I had been home a few months and couldn't find a job so I decided I had to leave. There was no way I was going to get myself together living in this desolate place.

I sat my daughters down, and told them I was leaving again, but this time it wouldn't be for long, and that I would come back to get all of them when I got on my feet.

We had gotten very close in a short period of time, and I knew they didn't really trust me because of my past, but I had to do something, so I called my probation officer and asked for a transfer.

A few weeks later I boarded a flight headed for Oakland, California to be with Samson, and to start a new life.

Samson helped me with everything; he taught me how to create a resume, and even bought me a nice business suit to wear when I looked for a job.

He taught me what to say, and what not to say in an interview. He told me to sit up straight, and look them directly in the eyes with confidence. He taught me power words to use when I spoke, and to avoid using hand gestures when I spoke. Samson was my savior.

I walked into the job fair for a national company called Frito Lay. There must have been hundreds of men there, and only a hand full of women. I was the only black woman there, and I stood out like a sore thumb, but I didn't care; I was in desperate need of a job and I had nothing to lose.

I walked into the elaborate conference room, and seated behind a big mahogany table, were a panel of six high powered executives. Before I took a seat; I introduced myself, and shook their hands like Samson told me to do. I gave them my fake resume with such pride; it was as if I'd really achieved everything I said I accomplished on that piece of paper.

They asked me questions about my former employment, and why I left, and I put on the performance of a lifetime. I told them that I worked in sales and distribution for many years, and that I had just relocated to the area. Which was somewhat the truth.

The next week I received a call from the recruiter offering me the job as an Account Sales Manager, earning six-hundred and fifty dollars a week salary, plus commission.

The job had benefits as well; medical, dental, 401k, and stocks in the company. I didn't know what half that stuff was, but I was excited, because I knew it had to be something good.

I wasn't there three months before I landed my dream job. When I got home, I fell to my knees, and began thanking God for granting me favor.

When Samson got home from work, we celebrated my new job over dinner. All I could think about was calling mama and the kids to share the good news. Mama always told me how bright I was, and that I could do anything I put my mind to, and I was starting to believe she was right.

I told Samson I had to get my kids, so that my life could be complete. He agreed to help me without any hesitation.

I wondered in the back of my mind why he wanted me with three kids and a lot of baggage; when he could have any woman he wanted without a readymade family.

When I asked him "Why me?" he said that he loved my loyalty, honesty and ambition. He said he was an only child, and he longed for brothers and sisters all his life. I told him that after we got married I'd give him a child of his own.

I wanted everything to be right when I got my kids, and I knew his tiny two bedroom house was too small for five people, so he agreed to buy me a house.

A month later we moved into a beautiful five bedroom house. It was a lease to own with an option to buy after two years. I was excited because the only house I ever lived in was my parents, and I was ready to build a home and a life with Samson, and my children.

Samson and I drove back to Southern California in the summer of nineteen-ninety-four to get my children. I knew Keith wouldn't let me take Michael if he knew I moved out of town, so I didn't tell him.

We met at the McDonald's like we always did; I asked if I could have Michael for the entire day so that I could take him shopping, and reluctantly, Keith agreed.

As soon as Keith was out of sight; Samson and I jumped in the car; went to my mother's house, picked up my youngest daughter Monica and left.

My oldest daughter Mya refused to come; she couldn't bear the thought of leaving mama. I didn't want to force her to come, so I let her stay.

I felt a sense of relief come over me once we made it home. I walked into our beautiful new house; with its white carpet, and spiral stairs; hand in hand with my two children.

I was so proud that day that I couldn't stop smiling. I took the kids to their appointed bedrooms, and watched as their faces lit up like a Christmas tree. They'd never had their own bed; much less their own bedroom.

I took them shopping, and let them pick out whatever they wanted for their bedroom. That night I cooked dinner, and we sat at the dining room table for the first time in our life, and ate dinner together.

That night I went in the backyard; looked in the sky at the moon and the stars, and I made a promise to God that I would give my life to him.

My life was starting to feel complete, and for once I felt like I'd done something right. I read my son a bedtime story; tucked him in bed, and as I walked past Monica's bedroom I could hear her sobbing. I went into her room to see what was wrong; I held her in my arms, and kissed her. She told me she missed Mama, and that she wanted to go home.

Sadness overwhelmed me, I thought to myself; how could I possibly think this was going to be easy? I knew had my work cut out for me, and I was determined to make things better for everyone involved. So every weekend I would load up the kids, and head for mamas' house so they could visit.

Slowly but surely things got better, and soon my oldest daughter Mya came to visit. Our relationship was strained at first. Sometimes when I didn't do something she wanted me to do, she would throw my past mistakes in my face.

The remorse I felt inside consumed me, and I found myself like putty in their hands. I did whatever they wanted to ease my guilt, because I didn't know what else to do. I knew they loved me; that's why they gave me a second chance, and I didn't want to disappoint them ever again.

I was climbing the corporate ladder fast and the number one sales manager for Frito Lay in Northern California retail market. I exceeded expectations every month. I was grossing eight to ten thousand dollars in commission alone and there was no stopping me.

I put kids in the best schools, brought them designer clothes, and I made sure they didn't want for anything. My head got so big that I forgot about God, and all the promises I'd made. I stopped going to church, I didn't pay my tides, or read my bible anymore.

I was caught up in world. I made a man, money and material things my God. I lost sight of what God had done for me, and the promises I made became null, and void. I never fathomed that making a promise to God that I didn't keep would cost me everything.

Chapter Seventeen

It All Came Crashing Down

My life was headed in the right direction. I was excelling in my career, I had a good man by my side, I was engaged to be married, and I finally had my children under my roof.

We lived in an exclusive neighborhood in a big beautiful house. We drove brand new cars, and I had money in the bank that was legal. For once in my life I was content.

Samson, and I had a wonderful relationship, and he seemed to love my kids. He was much more of a disciplinarian then I was when it came to the kids, but I thought that balanced things out. I did everything I could to please him, because I felt like I owed him for saving my life.

It all came crashing down on me in the winter of nineteen-ninety-five. I kept in touch with my friends in prison; especially my best friend Shanae.

We talked on the phone in code, and wrote letters to each other using assumed names; because one of the many conditions of my probation was that I was not allowed to have any contact with any known felons or an officer of the law. I knew if they found out they would violate me, and send me back to prison.

I would buy things Shanae needed, and Samson would sneak them into the prison. We had a full proof operation going and everything was running smoothly.

Shanae's family became my family, and when it was time for them to visit her they'd stay at my house; since the prison was only an hour away from where I lived. I thought everything in my life was perfect, but reality slapped me in the face once again.

It was a Tuesday evening when Shanae called unexpectedly. Normally she called on Friday's to give me an update on everything that happened during the week. I knew something was wrong because Shanae didn't sound like her usual; humorous self. She said that she had something important to tell me, and asked me to stop what I was doing, and sit down.

I didn't know what to expect, but I did as she instructed. She didn't beat around the bush with any small talk. Instead she was very serious when she told me that Samson was cheating on me with another inmate, and if that wasn't bad enough; he was being investigated by the fed's for rape.

I was in a state of shock and disbelief. I didn't want to accept the truth. I trusted this man with my life, my freedom, and my children. I was still on probation, and wasn't allowed to have any contact whatsoever with anyone from prison; including an officer and he knew what would happen to me if I disobeyed the rules.

My biggest nightmare had become real. I knew it was too good to be true. I just couldn't believe Samson would risk losing everything we had worked so hard to build for a piece of ass!

When Shanae finished telling me everything that was going on I cried harder than I ever had before. It broke me down to my knees and made me vomit. I couldn't believe it was happening again.

Samson was the first man that I'd allowed myself to trust in a very long time. He knew my story; everything I'd gone through in the past. He professed his undying love for me, and my children, and promised he would never do to me, what every other man had done in the past.

I let down my wall, and welcomed him into my life, and my children's life; only to get played again. Here I was bragging about my wonderful life to everyone in prison; all the while I was a joke and Samson was making a complete fool out of me.

Shanae made me swear not to say anything. I had to keep my word, and remain silent, because she was being loyal to me, but that was one of the hardest promises I'd ever made to anyone, and I cherished our friendship enough to keep my mouth shut as much as it hurt.

I didn't know what I was going to do. I didn't want to up root my children, and start all over again. This was the first stable living situation we'd ever had together. I knew it was a matter of time before the other shoe dropped, and I didn't want my children to be entangled in this mess, and end up in the system.

I had to come up with a plan to leave before I got myself caught up in Samson's bullshit. I pretended nothing was wrong, and played along with him for weeks; never saying a word about what I had learned. I must admit it was difficult, but I was thankful to Shanae for warning me, and I couldn't betray her trust.

Samson was a member of the National Guards. He told me that he was being deployed to Haiti to help in a cleanup mission, and that he'd be gone for six months. I didn't believe that either, I thought he was trying to make a run for it, and leaving me behind to hold the bag; until he showed me his military orders.

A week later Samson was gone. I searched the attic, and located his brief case that he attempted to hide. Inside I discovered documents from the Federal Bureau of Prison stating Samson was under investigation for misconduct?

It was just a matter of time before the Federal Marshalls came knocking at my door. I wasn't prepared to suffer the loss of my freedom again, and I damn sure wasn't going to risk losing my children.

I dreaded having to call mama again for help, but I had no one else. It wasn't like the girls had fathers beating down the door to see them, and I'd rather burn in hell then to hear Keith say; "I told you so". My family was all they had.

I told mama what happened, and she told me to bring the kids back home as soon as possible. I was embarrassed to disappoint my children again, but I knew we I had no choice considering the circumstances I was faced with.

 I sat my daughters down, and explained what was going on. I told them everything in detail, because I knew they were old enough to understand.

They were happy to go back to mama. Turns out they didn't like Samson at all. Monica told me he was mentally and emotionally abusive. I asked her why she never said anything to me, and she said; "because I just wanted to be with you".

The more I found out about Samson; the angrier I became. I could hear Lacy whispering devilish thoughts in my head. It was one thing for a man to mess with me; I could live with that, but I refused to allow a man to abuse my children, and he was going to pay!

I didn't bother telling son why we were moving, because I knew he wouldn't care, so I just told him we were going to visit his grandmother, and he was fine. I packed my kids personal belongings; along with as many of their toys as I could stuff in my trunk. I loaded them in my car, and drove them back to Southern California laughing and singing all the way.

My picture perfect life was just a photo in a frame. It dawned on me that the harder I reached for love and happiness the further it got away from me.

When I returned from mama's house I called my probation officer, and told her that I needed to transfer back to Southern California to take care of my sick mother. I knew it was a lie, and I prayed it wouldn't back fire on me. My probation officer told me that the process to transfer back was very complicated, and could take several months.

She warned me that if I was caught out of my jurisdiction I would be violated, and sent back to prison. I was under so much stress that any day I would get a knock on the door from the feds.

I was scared all the time, looking over my shoulder. I felt like I was back in the dope game, and I didn't like that feeling of fear. I was losing control, and the bottle of Hennessy was calling my name, and I answered.

I had stopped drinking hard liquor, and smoking cigarettes when I got out of prison. The most I drank was an occasional glass of wine because Samson didn't drink.

As I slowly watched my life fall apart I opened Pandora's Box and I unleashed the drinking and smoking demon that plagued me most of my life.

I started missing work because I was too hung over to wake up. Then one night I got caught drunk driving, and was hauled off to jail, and my driver's license was suspended for three months, and I was given a D.U.I.

When my job found out they fired me. I couldn't believe they could just get rid of me like that. After all I was their top dog in sales, but I soon learned either you're an asset or a liability.

I had become suicidal. I began drinking nonstop. I'd wake up with a drink and pass out with a drink. A few weeks later the doctors told me I needed surgery because I had a tumor in my uterus.

My life was spiraling out of control again, and I knew why. I forgot about God, and I was being punished for not keeping my promise.

Samson finally called me from Haiti after two months. He was in the middle of proclaiming his eternal love for me, and telling me just how much he missed me; when I told him I found his briefcase, and knew all about the federal investigation.

Suddenly all I heard was static. I thought he had passed out because he didn't say a word for several minutes.

He tried to plead his case, and deny everything, but it was no use. My only question to him was "Why?" I was a good woman; I worked hard, cooked and cleaned.

There was an abundance of sex, and there was nothing I wasn't willing to do to please him, like the time he told me about his anal exam, and how good it felt when the doctor put his finger in his butt. I went to the adult store; purchased a strap on dildo and did anal sex to him, because I truly loved him and wanted to satisfy him in every way.

It became painfully obvious that he was no longer in love with me; if he ever loved me at all. Maybe I was just a charity case or a project. I really didn't understand nor did I care anymore. I refused to cry in his presence, because I didn't want him to have the satisfaction of thinking he was worth my tears.

I didn't bother to share that I had lost my job, or that I needed surgery, because I didn't want his pity.

I thought I had everything I needed, but life's countless disappointments can surely drag you down the same path. I found myself alone; with no man, no money and no plan. The sad part was that it was my fault.

I was sick and tired of being sick and tired. I drank myself into oblivion every night because that was the only way to stop the voices in my head.

The electricity and water got cut off, so I lived in my twenty-five hundred square foot house, in the dark for weeks with barely any food or water.

I managed to find loose change by looting my closet, and rummaging through old purses. I broke into the kids' piggy banks, and used that money to buy alcohol, and cigarettes.

I didn't care if I didn't eat as long as I was drunk, and could forget everything. I was destitute, and at the end of my rope when I met a girl name Natalie.

My failed relationship with Samson had destroyed me mentally, and emotionally. I was miserable, and deeply depressed. I'd made up my mind I was through with men. I wasn't going to focus on love, or a relationship anymore. I was just going to have fun.

I drove down to Los Angeles after I'd finally received my unemployment check. I needed to get away from that empty house, so I could try to figure out my next move.

I left early Friday morning in hopes that I could get there before the evening traffic. I'd planned on seeing my kids; when I got a phone call from a friend inviting me to a gay club located on Pico called the "Catch One".

I really wanted to see what being a lesbian was like in the free world, so it didn't take much to convince me to go. The place was packed from wall to wall with women. Some looked just like men, and they seem to know how to party, and enjoy themselves.

They were holding hands; kissing, rubbing, and grinding on each other with no embarrassment. I was shocked, and turned on at the same time.

That's the night I met Natalie. She casually walked up to me and introduced herself. I could see she considered herself as the masculine dominant figure. She was about five feet nine, light skin with hazel eyes. She wore her hair slick back in a ponytail.

She was an attractive women with a lot of mannish features. She even had a light mustache, and was dressed like a man; wearing black slacks and a crisp blue shirt.

She had this sexy walk, and her tone of voice was reminiscent of a man. She was soft spoken, and laid back and could charm the skin off a snake.

As the night progressed she told me that she'd just got out of the same federal correctional facility I was in. She was sentenced to eighteen months for attacking the jury at her girlfriends sentencing when they found her guilty.

You would think I would have ended the conversation right there and ran for the boarder; knowing this broad had to be crazy; but I didn't.

I thought that was an act of real love. My husband let me take the fall, and I was the mother of his first born son, and he could care less about me going to prison.

She said she had just ended her long term relationship with her girlfriend, and was single. I wasn't looking for a relationship with a women, I just wanted to have some fun; so we exchanged numbers.

We talked on the phone almost every day for a month. She seemed cool, and her conversation was always interesting to say the least.

One day she showed up on my door step with no warning. I was stunned to see her standing there all smiles with two large suitcases.

I welcomed her in reluctantly when she told me that she wanted to surprise me. I must admit I was surprised. She said she could only stay a week, so I didn't think that would be a problem.

A week turned into a month. Things were great in the beginning, we had good chemistry because we both stayed drunk all the time. It seemed like the perfect dirty little secret until one day we were in the grocery store, and this fine man hit on me.

I must admit he looked good. He was tall, dark and handsome with a sexy smile. He reminded me of Blair Underwood. I made the mistake of smiling back, and that's when all hell broke loose.

She turned into a psycho. She began cursing, and talking loud; having a temper tantrum like a spoiled brat. I'd never told her I wasn't attracted to men anymore, but she had never been with a man, and hated the thought that I had.

I wasn't a lesbian in my mind; I was just open minded and experimenting. Security escorted us out the store because she tried to fight the man just for smiling at me.

I refused to display any public affection towards Natalie. There was no holding hands or hugging allowed. Sometimes I'd walk in front of her, because I was too ashamed of people pointing fingers, and whispering about us.

Every time she wanted to go somewhere I would make up an excuse, because I couldn't subject myself to such humiliation. The only place we could go publicly was the gay club.

Natalie despised the fact that I was ashamed of people knowing about us, but that was the only way I could be with her. She agreed to my conditions under direst, and I knew our special friendship was coming to an end.

I told Natalie I had children, and I could never disgrace them by openly becoming a lesbian. The other problem was my religion. I battled with what was instilled in me by the church, and that made what I was doing difficult for me, because I was told being gay was demonic and that I would burn in hell.

It was now winter nineteen-ninety-six; just a few days before Christmas. I decided I just couldn't coexist with Natalie anymore. My conscience was bothering me, and I was consumed with guilt.

Natalie had become so possessive, and controlling that I couldn't take it anymore. She was drunk more than she was sober. I was tired of the mind games, and theatrics, so I told her it was over, and asked her to leave.

She seemed to grasp the news rather well, and pretended to accept my decision with no debate. She announced that she'd be on the first flight back to southern California the next morning. I was relieved that the conversation went so well, after all; Natalie was usually very confrontational, and would rather fight opposed to discussing anything rationally.

I was a bit surprised at how well she handled the news, but I decided not to look a gift horse in the mouth. I went downstairs to talk to Alexis; who'd come to visit a few days earlier. We'd planned to drive back to L.A. together, so I could spend Christmas with my children.

Alexis didn't agree with me seeing Natalie at all. She expressed her animosity countless times, and even stopped speaking to Natalie. I told Alexis I'd ended the dysfunctional relationship, and that Natalie was leaving, when suddenly I heard a blast that sounded like a cannon.

Alexis, and I looked at each other with the look of utter fear, because the sound we heard was a gun going off. I kept a twelve gauge rifle under my bed for protection. All I could envision was Natalie committing suicide. We both ran up the stairs towards my bedroom, and when I threw open the French doors; there stood Natalie.

She was topless wearing only boxer shorts. Her hair was all over her head, and she was holding the twelve gauge rifle pointing it directly at us. She looked like Jack Nicholson in the movie "The Shining". Alexis turned around and ran downstairs to get her daughter. I stood there in shock, frozen in fear, with my hands up in the air as though I was under arrest.

I tried to reason with Natalie. She was so inebriated you could smell the alcohol seeping through her pores. She was crying, and slurring her words. She kept repeating "I love you Raven" over and over. I didn't know what to do. She had crushed my cell phone into pieces, and snatched the landline cord out of the wall.

She pointed the gun directly in my face and said "If I can't have you, I'm going to kill you". I asked her if we could sit down for a moment so we could talk about it, and after a few minutes of convincing she backed up towards the bed.

We both sat on the edge of the mattress, and it was silence at first. I glanced around my once elegant master bedroom, and saw that she had blasted my bathroom mirrors off, and there was a gaping hole in the wall. You could see the next door neighbor's house.

Alexis yelled to me from downstairs that she was leaving. She wanted me to come with her, but I was in fear that Natalie would try to shoot me in the back if I attempted to leave, and possibly hurt Alexis, and her daughter, so I told her to go.

I tried my best to calm Natalie down, so I could get the gun away from her, but it was as if she was possessed. One minute she would be relaxed, and passive, and the next minute she'd be violent and aggressive. She kept drinking vodka straight from the bottle, and the more she drank the worse it got.

She became physically abusive; slapping me in my face, and

grabbing my arms. Natalie was as strong as any man I'd ever encountered, so it was hard for me to keep up with her. I threw lamps, and hit her with furniture, and she kept coming.

I managed to get down the stairs when she turned to grab the rifle, and I made it outside. She came outside half naked with the rifle screaming my name as I hid in the neighbors bushes. She walked the perimeter of my house for over an hour, and then finally went back inside.

I stayed in the bushes, freezing with no shoes on until the sun came up, then when I felt she was asleep; I tip toed into the house through the garage, I managed to locate my extra set of car keys that I kept hidden underneath the car. I jumped into my car bear feet, dirty, and cold and started the engine. I let the garage door up, and turned to look behind me, so I could back out safely. I thought I was home free; when suddenly I heard something hit the hood of my car.

When I turned around; Natalie was lying on the hood of my car staring at me like a crazed psychopath. I raved up the engine, and instructed her to get off the car, but she refused. My patience had run out and I didn't care anymore. I felt a sense of rage take over me, so I took off down the street with the crazy bitch hanging from the hood like an ornament!

It felt like the twilight zone outside. It was seven o' clock on a Saturday morning, and I couldn't find a soul on foot or driving by. I drove down the street as fast as I could, then hit the brakes to throw her off my car.

When I saw her hit the ground; I backed up, and went around her, and drove off. I looked in my rearview mirror, and saw that she was still lying there motionless. I was afraid that I'd killed her, so I turned around, and went back to check. I couldn't live with that on my conscience, and I wasn't that heartless and cruel.

When I got out the car I could hear her moaning, and groaning, I walked over to her; put her head in my lap, and asked her if she could move. I lifted her from the ground, and carried her around her waist, and put her in the back seat of my car.

She laid there lifeless, and all I could think was at least she's quiet for once. I was so scared she was going to die, I didn't know what to do, so I just drove home.

When we got home I dragged her out of the car and we both crawled into the house looking like we had just gotten out of the ring with Floyd MayWeather.

Natalie knew it was over between us, and a few days later, I drove her to the airport in silence, she boarded a plane back to southern California without a fight.

I thought things ended rather well considering everything that happened prior to her leaving, but I understood I was dealing with an obsessed; crazy lesbian, and I just didn't know what to expect next.

I should have known she wasn't finished with me yet. Turns out Natalie found out where my parents lived from looking through my mail, and showed up at their door.

She had the nerve to tell my mother that she was in love with me; that I was her girlfriend and that we were in a lesbian relationship for a year.

When I found out what she'd done; I lost it! I wanted to kill her for exposing me to my family. That was the straw that broke the camel's back! I got a restraining order against her to ensure she stayed away from me, and my family.

Natalie stalked me like a predator for months. Then one day she just disappeared. I didn't hear from her, and she didn't pop up anywhere I was.

I could feel a sense of relief come over me, and I was glad that she'd finally given up. A year had passed, and one day out of the blue she called me from a blocked number.

She told me she was in the hospital; suffering from liver failure, and that she was dying. I didn't know what to say or how to feel. I sat quietly, and listened to the weary voice on the other end of the phone.

She wanted me to come visit her in the hospital, but I was afraid of her; I thought it was another plot of hers to try to get me. I never went to the hospital, and I ever heard from Natalie again.

Years have passed, and I often wondered if she died. I tried to find her on the vast social media networks just to see if she was still alive, but I could never find any information on her so I assume she passed away.

In my eyes; Natalie was a tortured soul like me, and I knew that by the way she treated herself. She wanted love like we all do, and she didn't know how to accept rejection.

I gave up that lifestyle. I told myself that wasn't what God had in planned for me. I might as well stay with a man rather than be with a woman pretending to be a man, and treating me worst then a man. I thought at least God wouldn't frown on me for doing that anymore.

It took six months for the probation department to approve my transfer, and in January nineteen-ninety-seven I reluctantly packed my bags, rented a U-Haul, and took everything in the house; leaving Samson nothing but his briefcase, and what was left of his clothes that I'd burned up in a fit of rage.

I drove back to Southern California alone. I had no blueprint, and no plan for the future. All I knew was that I'd failed again.

Chapter Eighteen

Starting Over From Scratch

It was the winter of nineteen-ninety-seven, it took a while, but I managed to get back on my feet with the help of God, and my parents. I went in the hospital, and my surgery was a success. I was ready to conquer the world.

I finally found a job after months of searching. It didn't pay much, but it beat welfare. In a matter of months my children, and I moved into an apartment. It was a far cry from the big beautiful house I had in San Francisco, but I was thankful just to have a place to call my own.

I was tired of sending my kids back to my parents every time things in my life took a dive, but I was blessed to have the type of parents who welcomed me, and my children with open arms every time I needed help.

My oldest daughter Mya was now seventeen; graduating from high school. Monica was fifteen, and Michael was ten. Things were good between us, and we had grown closer. They had begun to trust me a little, but something was still missing in my life.

Alexis and I grew apart. She was still my best friend, but she lived several hours away so I didn't see her much anymore. The last adventure we had was when her baby's father Darryl sent us plane tickets to come visit him in New York in the summer of nineteen-ninety-six.

When we arrived he put us up in the Hilton hotel near the airport. He took us to dinner and a comedy show. I could see he was trying his best to impress me, granted he was really nice, but he very boring. He worked in the music industry and bragged about all the famous people he knew. That didn't empress me at all, they were rich and famous and he wasn't.

Alexis wasn't interested in him anymore, but an all-expense paid trip made her tolerate him for seven days. The next night Alexis, and I figured out a way to ditch him so we could hit up some clubs.

As soon as we walked through the door of the club; all the men were on us. Maybe it was because we were half naked, wearing short miniskirts and low cut skimpy tops that left nothing to the imagination.

We weren't there five minutes before Alexis caught the eye of this fine ass baller sitting in the VIP section. He sent her a drink like most classy men would do and asked her to join him.

Alexis was use to the finer things in life. She'd grown up in a nice home with nannies and maids. She had traveled the world and had seen places I'd only dreamed of.

She grabbed my arm and pulled me to towards the VIP section. There were several other half naked girls there along with a few other men. The Champagne was flowing which was right up Alexi's alley, because that's all she drank.

I felt out of place, because everyone seemed to be coupled up, and I was just a third wheel, so I walked to the bathroom just to get away.

On my way back I was greeted by this handsome man who offered to buy me a drink. I must admit I was shocked, this kind of thing never happened to me before, and the men in Los Angeles definitely didn't buy drinks for anyone but themselves.

He introduced himself as Adam, and told me he was a New York City police officer. At first I was intimidated because of my past encounters with the law, but I just went along with him knowing it wouldn't result in anything meaningful.

Adam, and I had been dancing all night, and when the club closed he invited me to breakfast. Alexis declined the offer because the rich baller she'd been with all night requested the honor of her presence to join him, and his friends for breakfast, so we parted ways with plans of catching up with each other before we went back to the hotel.

It was now five am, and I was beat. I called Alexis who still wasn't ready to go back to the hotel, so Adam was kind enough to let me come to his apartment to wait. He was such a gentleman. He made me some coffee, and let me sleep in his bed while he slept on the couch. Around noon Alexis called, and we met up, and headed back to the hotel to face Darryl.

As soon as we opened the door to our hotel room, there was Darryl; pacing back and forth on his cell phone. He was furious; eyes bulging, hands flying in the air; pointing directly at us.

He was saying something, because his lips were moving, but Alexis, and I were still intoxicated, and incoherent, so all we could do was laugh.

We tried to ignore him; hoping he would just shut up, and leave, but instead he kept going on, and on; until finally Alexis couldn't take it anymore, and it developed into a heated argument.

The biggest mistake he made was getting in her face, and pushing her. I'd never seen anything like that before. Alexis started hyperventilating, her eyes grew wide, and she was yelling at the top of her lungs, and before I knew it; she'd lost complete control.

She was swinging on him like Mike Tyson. She picked up a floor lamp, and hit him with it. They struggled towards the balcony, and he threatened to throw her off if she didn't stop hitting him.

The last thing I recall is him begging me to call security to get her off of him. That was the first time I'd ever seen a women beat a man before; it was hilarious, and frightening at the same time.

Alexis beat him senseless. I thought to myself; I wish I could have done that to Keith. Alexis, and I had an unspoken bond that most people didn't understand. The fact of the matter was; I could be myself with her, and she could be herself with me.

There was no pride or shame between us, we shared everything, and exposed ourselves to each other without fear of being judged. I told her things I'd never told anybody else, and no matter how farfetched our ideas were; we supported each other.

When I told her I was sleeping with Keith from time to time, she didn't criticize me, even though she despised him for everything he'd done to me.

I always felt like I needed to have someone in my life regardless of how they treated me. I don't know why I felt this way, I just did.

Keith, and I would sneak around to have sex, because we didn't want anyone to know; especially our son. Keith had done well for himself, he had a good job, his own house, and a young girlfriend. I didn't care about her, and I didn't think it was wrong because we were still married.

I often wondered when his day to reap would come. I couldn't accept the fact that he had a better life than me. He seemed happy, and content, and I loathed it. I kept waiting for the other shoe to drop, but it never did. So I took what I could get, but deep inside I wanted him to beg me to take him back, but that never happened.

After all he had done to me; I didn't know why I wanted him to still want me. Maybe it was because I didn't love myself enough to know that I deserved better.

I asked Keith why he did all the things he'd done to me. He looked at me with this look of amazement, and said, "Because you loved me too much!" I had no response for that answer. I thought to myself "When did loving someone too much become a crime?"

He went on to tell me that he lost respect for me because I loved him more then I loved myself, and that I had no self-esteem, and didn't value myself. That was a bitter pill to swallow, and the after taste was even worse.

Keith always did love himself more than he loved me, or any- body else for that matter. When we were together he had to have his own bathroom, and would spend hours in the mirror gazing at himself saying, "I love you" as though he was talking to someone else.

I thought he was just conceited, but I realize that he was pleased, and satisfied with the reflection staring back at him in the mirror. My only wished was that I felt the same way about myself.

I thought about everything Keith said that day. I tried to change, but something inside me wouldn't allow me to relinquish the doubts I had about who I was, or what I deserved. I didn't know how to love myself, because I didn't know who I was.

I had countless failed relationships after Samson. Every man I'd ever been involved with cheated on me. It didn't matter how fine I was, how freaky I was in bed, or how good I could cook. They just couldn't be fateful to me.

I even lowered my standards, and accepted men who I wasn't even attracted to, and who had nothing whatsoever to offer me, and they still cheated. I had begun to think I was meant to be in this world alone.

Alexis had men falling at her feet. It seemed the worse she treated them; the more they loved her! I tried to be a gold digging bitch like Shellie, but that just wasn't me.

I was that ride or die chick always down with the underdog. I always had their backs, and tried to help build them up. I always felt sorry for them the minute they told me a sob story or shed a tear, I'd give them my all, and each time I did; I was left standing in the cold.

I was weak, my vision was unclear, and I couldn't trust my own intuition. I had no confidence, and I'd lost sight of who I really was, or what I really wanted from a man. I didn't even know why I wanted a man. It wasn't as if there was anything great about them. They didn't make me feel good in any way, shape or form.

They didn't wine, and dine me, or spoil me rotten. All they did was take from me. Physically they destroyed my body with their abuse. Mentally they destroyed my mind with their games. Emotionally they played with my feelings, with their cheating and their lies. Financially they robbed me of everything I had, and never gave me anything in return.

Growing up I was taught a women was supposed to have a man, so that's what I asked God to send me. Maybe I should have been more descriptive in my request, because all I got was a man, and some of them were questionable. They were a far cry from the man my father was. None of them knew the first thing about how to treat a woman.

Most of them were selfish, and self-centered; and cared only for themselves. They had no respect for me; didn't value my contributions, or the sacrifices I'd made in the relationship.

I made the mistake of making them feel they were more important than me. I put them on a pedestal; made them my God, and that is where I made my biggest mistake.

I thought loving them was enough. I thought helping them showed my dedication, and commitment. I thought they would recognize that I was a good woman, and do anything possible to have me in their life; but they never did.

Several years had passed, and I'd been in, and out of more failed relationships than I cared to remember. For some reason every man I attracted had a prison record. It was like they were magnets, and I was a piece of metal.

I thought I couldn't break that cycle until I met Gerald. We met after I broke up with Samson. Gerald was from Oakland, California. We encountered each other in the grocery store one day while searching for some fruit.

Gerald was attractive even though he was short. He stood about five feet-eight inches, and was dark skin, with long hair down his back. He had tight sleepy eyes that made him appear high all the time, but he didn't smoke marijuana or use any type of drugs.

I really liked Gerald because he was very determined and ambitious, and he wasn't an ex-convict. Gerald wasn't a bad boy; he'd never even had a speeding ticket. He would cook dinner for me; take me to nice restaurants, and night spots.

Gerald was very positive. He was a good father to his children, and that really impressed me; since none of my children had a relationship with their fathers.

He told me he was a music producer, but I'd never heard of him. He always bragged about how big he was going to be in the industry one day and I liked that he believed in himself.

He had his own place, nice car and he dressed immaculate. He loved to do adventurous things like mountain climbing and hiking; something none of the other black men I dated would ever think of doing.

We dated for several months, and things were going great with the exception of his baby Mama drama. He had four children by two different women. It seemed every other day he was arguing with one of them over something.

Once I stayed the weekend at his house. It was early Saturday morning; we had been up most of the night drinking, partying and having sex.

The doorbell rang around seven am, and Gerald jumped up to answer it. I stayed in bed waiting for him to return; then suddenly I could hear a female's voice in the distance.

I put on my robe, and sat on the side of the bed for a minute because I wasn't sure who it was, and I didn't want to jump to any conclusions.

I could hear their voices become louder, and louder, and by the time I reached the living room the woman was inside the house, and she was breaking wine glasses and swinging on Gerald.

I didn't understand what was going on. This woman whom I'd never seen before; stood before me yelling and screaming. She was in tears calling Gerald as a liar and a cheater.

She blurted out obscenities to me, calling me a bitch; whore, and a home wrecker. I refused to allow her to disrespect me, and just when I was about to let her have it; I found out she was Gerald's baby Mama.

She informed me that they were still involved in an ongoing relationship, and that they had been together four years. She introduced herself as Stacie, and shoved her ring finger in my face; informing me that they were engaged to be married.

I glanced at Gerald who stood there looking like a complete and utter fool. I gracefully apologized to his fiancée; walked into the bedroom, packed my bags, took a shower, and left without saying a word. That was the last time I saw Gerald.

I knew how it felt to be lied to, and cheated on, and I refused to be the other woman. I soon figured out no man was exempt from lying and cheating.

It was the summer of nineteen-ninety-nine when Gerald found me in Southern California. He wrote me this long letter claiming he hired a private detective to look for me because he just couldn't get me out of his mind, and he wanted to apologize to me in person. All the while I was thinking "why did it take two years?"

Gerald flew down to Ontario Airport on a Saturday evening and we met for dinner. He claimed that the relationship with his daughter's mother was over, and convinced me that he really wanted to be with me.

I was so flattered. After all no man had ever shown that much interest in me to hire someone to find me, so I fell for it; hook, line and sinker.

Things between us were good for a while, and after a few

months of commuting back, and forth between Los Angeles and Oakland he finally mustered up the nerve to tell me what he really wanted from me.

I should have known there was a catch; because things like this just didn't happen to me. I couldn't believe it when he asked me to help him pull off a heist.

The once good guy had turned bad. I guess his producing skills didn't pan out, and he was struggling to make ends meet and thought I would be the idiot to bail him out.

I knew I slipped up by revealing too much information about myself to him. That was one of my biggest downfalls, I trusted the wrong people and I talked too much!

Once he learned I'd been to federal prison, I guess he assumed I was a prime candidate for the job. I played along with him for a few weeks; leading him to believe I was down.

I had him wining and dining me, sending me money and when I got tired of playing the game I called him and told him I didn't want to do it.

As quickly has he appeared back in my life; he disappeared, and his love for me turned into animosity, and our relationship was over which was fine with me.

I had vowed that I would never lose my freedom for another man again. That was the one time I chose logic over love, and I had no regrets.

Gerald was no different than all the rest of the sorry men I'd encountered. He tried to use me because he could sense my vulnerability, and my lack of self-confidence.

I made the mistake of sharing my whole life story with anybody who would listen; thinking they would have compassion, and understanding. They didn't care about me or my struggles. All they did was utilize it for personal gain, and when they got what they wanted out of me; they discarded me like yesterday's newspaper.

I had to figure out the secret to life's happiness. I wanted to know how some people found the love of their life; got married, stayed together, and live happily ever after until the day one of them died.

Whatever I was doing wasn't working in my favor, and I couldn't seem to discover what I was doing wrong. I knew there had to more to life than this. I just didn't know how to seize the moment. I wanted to feel what it felt like to be loved for once in my life.

Chapter Nineteen

Another Bad Choice

The new Millennium was just a month away. I was praying that things would get better for me. My thirty-ninth birthday was slowing approaching, and I was still absent of happiness, and true fulfillment in my life. I never imagined life would be this difficult for so long.

I'd worked my way up to a Collection Manager in just two years, and was working for a large company in Riverside, California. This was the first position I had in a long time that held a title that commanded respect, and I was proud of my achievements.

I tried to look out for anyone who needed a job. I hired as many blacks as I could, and although all the other managers thought I was crazy, I didn't forget where I came from, and it was important for me to try to give them a chance, because somebody believed in me and gave me a chance.

Most of the people I hired were loyal, and dedicated to me, they praised, and worshiped the ground I walked on, and that made me feel important. It made me to feel good to help someone else.

The time had come for our company Christmas party. Most of the women at the job were married; even the ugly; fat women had husbands. I was still single, I didn't even have a boyfriend. They'd always ask me why I didn't have a man, but I'd lie and say it was by choice. I assumed they must have done something right, because they had husbands, and had been married for years.

I begin thinking to myself, "their husbands must be cheating" because these women were not the pick of the litter. Most of them didn't know how to dress to flatter their bodies, and wore little to no makeup. They looked homely to me. Then it dawned on me that maybe that's why they had a husband.

I decided to take my cousin Patricia with me to the Christmas party just so I wouldn't walk in alone. We always had fun when we were together, and I thought what better person to have with me then my beautiful, sexy cousin.

We arrived at the Military base where the celebration was held at nine pm. The band was playing some boring elevator music, and the ballroom was filled with big round tables; with red table cloths, and fine China. We were escorted to the managers table. Where I was surrounded by these stuffy couples pretending to be happy.

I could tell some of the women were intimidated by Patricia and I, and it was amusing to say the least. Patricia was always a social butterfly so she quickly began to mingle. I was uncomfortable sitting with the other managers, and their spouses so I joined my team, and socialized with them. They were all in their twenties, and they knew how to have fun.

They were laughing, dancing, and taking shots of tequila, and after fraternizing for a while I contemplated that it was time to join the other managers so it wouldn't seem as though I was being rude. I walked to the bar to order a drink when I saw a man glaring at me, undressing me with his eyes.

I returned to my seat, and the stranger calmly walked over, and introduced himself as Jonathan. He was the son of my colleague Alberta. I'd known her for a few years, and she'd never mentioned this son before.

He was tall; light skin, with freckles. He had sparkly white teeth, and a sexy smile. He had a boyish like charm, and a body that looked as though it was chiseled out of stone. He resembled Shamar Moore the actor.

He looked rather young, and I was stunned when he said he was thirty-five. I'd run across men like him before, and past experience taught me not to trust men that looked that good again.

The more I drank the easier it was for me to find his flirting cute. We danced all night, and when the party was over he escorted me to my car. We exchanged phone numbers, and parted ways.

We talked on the phone a few times but and I wasn't going to let myself get caught up. Jonathan was very persistent. No matter how many times I told him I wasn't interested in a relationship he kept calling. He wouldn't give up and he wouldn't take no for an answer. Soon I found myself talking to him on a regular basis. He finally confided in in me about his past and when I found out he had just gotten out of prison after serving seventeen years; I was ready to run in the opposite direction fast.

He laid this sad sob story on me about how he got in trouble as a youth and was charged as an adult for drugs. I realized that he'd spent half of his life in prison. He was just seventeen years old when he got locked up. No wonder Alberta never mentioned him. All I could think of was; "Why me?"

I should have put on my tennis shoes, and ran for the hills, but I didn't. I got involved with him in a moment of weakness. I felt sorry for him, because he grew up in prison, and didn't know how to do anything.

He told me that he wasn't close to his mother, and that she never wrote him, or came to visit. The more he talked the sorrier I felt for him. I started to dislike his mother for abandoning her child when he needed her the most. My mother would never do that to me.

Jonathan didn't know simple things like; how to use a microwave, DVD player, or a washing machine; things that I took for granted were like rocket science for Jonathan.

He'd never had a bank account, or written a check before. He didn't have any form of credit, and didn't know what a fico score was.

I immediately embraced him, and thought I had to save him. After a brief romance we moved in together after knowing each other for only three of months.

His mother and I worked together, and she appeared to be a nice women, so I thought he couldn't be so bad. I should have thought about the fact that my mother was a nice woman too, and look how I turned out, but I didn't.

Four months into the relationship, I found out Jonathan had been going through my cell phone; anonymously calling my friends trying to solicit them to have a threesome with us.

When I heard the news I confronted him, and he gave me this heartbreaking story about how he'd spent most of his life in prison, and that he'd missed out on so much. He claimed he was just curious.

Jonathan was pathetic, and I felt bad for him. I forgave him, and after a while he convinced me to have a threesome with him for his birthday present. I blamed myself for telling him about the beautiful lesbian at my job who was hitting on me, and for revealing my past sexual encounters with women.

I felt like he had been cheated out of so much living, that maybe he should experience this with me, so like a fool, I surrendered.

The thought of a threesome turned Jonathan on. I can't say I felt the same way, I had my reservations only because I'd had a threesome and the outcome didn't end well.

I was skeptical about doing that again, but Jonathan was unrelenting, and promised me that once he'd experienced having a threesome it would be out of his system.

I informed Jonathan about the rules. No kissing her in the mouth, and no oral sex with her. I knew she didn't prefer men, and that she was only doing it because she wanted to be with me. When I called Lydia she accepted the offer immediately. We agreed to meet at my house that Saturday night at seven pm.

My son had gone to Keith's house for spring break. Lydia arrived promptly at seven. In the back of my mind I wanted to back out of it, because I knew deep down inside that I couldn't stand the thought of watching my man have sex with another women. I turned on some music, and took a few shots of Hennessy to calm my nerves.

In my youth I was down for anything ,but I found that the older I got the less interested I was in wild meaningless sex. I wanted a monogamous relationship with one person who I loved and who loved only me. Yet here I was nearly forty behaving like I was twenty to please a man.

We went into the bedroom, and at first Jonathan just wanted to watch Lydia have sex with me. After a while he joined in, and climbed on top of me first.

We were kissing, and making love for about fifteen minutes. Lydia was rubbing my face and caressing my breasts. Then Jonathan switched from me to her. He climbed on top of her, and begin having sex with her. I laid next to them in the bed, and watched. I could s oftygment>

see how much he was enjoying it by the way he was moaning and groaning.

I got out of bed and sat in a chair across the room, and for twenty minutes I intensely watched as Jonathan was stroking up and down, never noticing that I was even gone. Then he broke the rules!

He started kissing her in the mouth passionately, then he went down on her. I couldn't believe it. She looked at me with a smirk on her face as though to say "I told you so", and before I knew it, I'd marched into the kitchen, grabbed the biggest butcher knife I could find, and ran back into the room and began stabbing.

They both jumped out of bed, and stood there butt naked, begging me to put down the knife. The night ended with me throwing both of them out of my house.

Jonathan continued to call for weeks; begging me to forgive him, and to let him come home, but I had enough. I lowered myself for him, and that was how he repaid me. I realized he couldn't be trusted, and that I owed him nothing. It wasn't my fault he spent seventeen years in prison, and it wasn't my duty to save him.

A few weeks had passed, and Jonathan had stopped calling. I was relieved that he'd finally given up, and I was ready to move on with my life. Things were tense at work, because his mother Alberta, and I weren't speaking anymore.

She got mad at me for throwing his sorry ass out on the street. It didn't matter to me what she thought; after all she'd left him for dead in prison according to Jonathan, so how could she judge me for my decision?

She did everything in her power to get me fired from my job, and eventually it worked. I was terminated after she told the director that I'd been in prison, and failed to disclose that information on my job application. I guess that's what I deserved for talking too much. I'd pillow talked with Jonathan about my past, and he shared that information with his mother to use against me.

I later learned that Jonathan was arrested again for credit card fraud, and sentenced to eight years in federal prison. I guess he couldn't adapt to the free world after all.

A few years later I found out Jonathan was a registered sex offender

165

on Megan's Law and had served time in prison for rape, and other disgusting acts.

To top it off I ran into a friend who had been is state prison and he said that Jonathan was in the closet and that he messed around with fags in prison for years! Looks are deceiving, and I was blinded by his outer appearance, his good looks and tone body made me believe he was a real man.

Jonathan wanting to have freaky sex with multiple women hid his double life and his lust for men from me. I guess that's the disguise he used to fool me.

I nearly lost my mind! What was I thinking? I couldn't believe my poor judgment; I never checked out his story. I took him at face value just like I did with all the other men in my life.

I opened the door for the devil, and welcomed a gay; sex offender into my home with me, and my children.

I was so desperate to have a man; any man, that I didn't even stop to find out anything about him.

I was thankful that he never did anything to my children, because I would have ended up back in prison for murder, but it was mama's prayers, and God's grace that protected them, not me.

I decided from that moment on that I wouldn't live my life that way again. I refused to allow another man's circumstances to become my problem.

I made up my mind not to trust any man and especially a man who had spent his life in prison. Every man was suspect in my eyes and not to be trusted.

I had a sob story too, but I never made anyone feel obligated to save me. I was open an honest about my past, I didn't pretend to be something that I'm not just to get a man or woman in bed. I sucked it up; all the anger and rage I felt inside and I kept it pushing because I had no choice.

Chapter Twenty

Til Death Do Us Part

It was August 2001, six months had passed since I'd ended my relationship with Jonathan. I needed extra money so I went to work for my sister, and her husband at their restaurant on the weekends.

I wasn't looking for anyone when I met Rodney. He was a cook, and busboy. Like every man I attracted he had just served twelve years in prison for selling drugs, and claimed he had turned his life around.

Rodney was nothing close to the kind of man I dreamed of. He was short; standing at five foot-nine. He had dark skin, a big nose and wore his hair in a long ponytail. He had eight metal pins in his knee and walked with a limp because he'd been shot in the during a botched drug deal back in the eighties.

Rodney was big, and buffed, but he had a squeaky little voice that reminded me of Mike Tyson. His arms were covered in Tattoo's. Most of them were gang related, but he attempted to cover them up when he was released from prison.

He had different women's names tattooed on his chest. I often wondered what a woman had to do to be worthy enough for a man to burn her name into his flesh. In my eyes that was the ultimate confirmation that a man loved you.

My name had never been burned on a man's body, so I knew I was never anyone special to a man.

Rodney was a retired gang member from Compton. He had four kids by three different women. We became friends, and would talk to each other about our lives, and our past relationships all the time.

He told me he was a single father raising his oldest son, trying to make it. He wasn't my type at all, but then again who was? At this point I really had no clue.

Rodney told me he was the youngest boy of thirteen siblings, and he was originally from Chicago. He presented himself as a decent person who just made mistakes in life, and because of my checkered past I could relate to that since I felt the same way.

I really didn't like Rodney in a sexual way, but loneliness will make you do crazy things, and one thing led to another, and I found myself spending more, and more time with Rodney.

He was fairly intelligent for an ex-gang member. He told me he'd attended two years at community college for accounting before he joined the gang.

He said the death of his mother landed him in the streets because he never knew his father, and had no positive role models. Rodney seemed nice, and tried hard to convince me that he had a little bit of class, although I could see that he really didn't.

One day he invited me over to his house for dinner, and drinks. At the time I was out of work, living with my sister, and things in my life were downhill again. My spirits were low, so I accepted his offer. He lived in a two bedroom condo, it wasn't the best place I'd ever been, but it wasn't the worst place either.

I knew he was struggling, his furniture was old, and worn out. It looked like it was from the seventies. I thought to myself at least he had a place to stay. We sat down to have dinner at his beat up old dining room table with its three chairs. He served me an elegant dinner, consisting of Lamb, red potatoes and green beans. I must admit it was pretty good.

When we finished eating Rodney asked if I wanted to watch a movie, and I agreed. I followed him down the hall into his bedroom. That furniture looked to be from the seventies too. The dresser was this big wood monstrosity with shelves, and light sconces in it. It had several water rings from where someone had sat a wet glass. He had a big king size bed, with a mattress that had seen better days.

When I sat down I could feel the metal springs sticking me in my butt whenever I moved, so I tried to sit in one spot. He poured me a glass of cheap wine, and I was surprised that he even had wine glasses. He pulled out a bunch of bootleg movies, and as we shuffled threw them, I heard a knock on his bedroom door.

It was his sixteen year old son. He introduced us, and then his son asked him for a "blunt." He told him where to find them, and he went on his way. I sat there in amazement at what I'd just witnessed. I thought to myself "What the hell is going on here?" I didn't smoke weed anymore, but I sure as hell knew what a blunt was. As wild as I was I'd never allowed my children to party with me or use drugs, and I could never understand parents who smoked weed and partied with their children.

I must admit I did let my children taste a sip of a wine cooler once, but that was just to keep them from sneaking them out of the refrigerator when they were teenagers. When I let them do it they informed me they didn't like it, and unlike me; I never had a problem with them drinking alcohol.

When it was time to go we walked into the living room. He turned on the light so I could get my coat, and all I saw were roaches scurrying around everywhere.

It was like we were under attack. My mouth hung open in a state of disbelief. All I could think about was that plate of food I'd just eaten, and my mouth started to water as if I were going to throw up.

I thought where in the hell were they hiding? I didn't know what to say, so I pretended not to notice. I grabbed my jacket, and said goodnight. When I got to my car I started shaking my jacket viciously to make sure I was taking any roaches home with me. I felt so bad for him because he really tried his best to impress me.

The next day he called, and asked me out again. Was he really that stupid? That's the thought that crossed my mind, but then I said to myself "at least he got a place to live, roaches and all". We went out a few days later to his sister's house. I was a little reluctant at first, but when we pulled up to her big beautiful house in the hills I couldn't imagine her having roaches.

A month passed, and I'd started my new job. I was trying to save enough money to move into my own place. My son and I were staying with my sister Tina temporarily, but she refused to give me a key. She claimed she didn't give out keys because then people would never leave.

I commuted over an hour each direction to work. I worked the swing shift so by the time I got home it would be late in the evening. Sometimes I had to sleep in my car because I'd be locked out of the house. Tina didn't have a landline phone, and sometimes when I'd knocked on the door she claimed she didn't hear me because her room was located in the back of the apartment.

I knew she really didn't want us there, and I didn't want to be there either, but I had nowhere else to go. My son was now twelve and had a broken leg, and couldn't walk. It was the summer, and he was out of school, and we needed a place to stay for a few months. I found myself sleeping in car more than I was sleeping in her house because most of the time I couldn't get in.

I told Rodney what I was going through, and he kindly offered to let us stay with him and his son. He even offered to give us his bedroom and sleep on the couch.

I thought that was such a sweet gesture, but I couldn't imagine living in that roach infested place. I grew up with roaches and I hated it then, the thought just made me cringe.

A few weeks went by and things at my sister house weren't getting any better, so Rodney kept insisting that I take him up on his offer. I told him I'd consider moving in if he got the place exterminated. I didn't know any other way to say it. He agreed, and after I was sure every four legged living creature in the house that couldn't speak English was dead; my son and I moved in.

Things were going good between Rodney, and I. Although his son was a few years older than my son, they got along great. I had my concerns because I knew his son smoked marijuana and I didn't want my son exposed to it.

They managed to find a few things in common even though his son already had a baby with some little white girl.

We made things work, and as the days flew by I found myself really caring for Rodney. We stayed together for three months, when he told me he loved me. I was convinced I was in love too. I told him I was never leaving and that I didn't want to live in sin, so we decided to get married.

Three months later I found myself in a little chapel in front of a few of our family and friends jumping the broom. Daddy walked me down the aisle reluctantly. He had his reservations about Rodney because he knew him from working with him at the restaurant, and he didn't think he was good enough for me.

Daddy looked so handsome in his black tuxedo and crisp white shirt. I felt honored because I was the only daughter my father had given away. I think if he had a choice he wouldn't have given me to Rodney.

The nuptials were short, and sweet, and the reception was as ghetto as they come. Rodney had every thug from Compton in the wedding party. Their eyes were bloodshot red, and they all smelled of weed, and alcohol.

The reception was held in his sister backyard because Rodney was cheap, and refused to rent a reception hall. To top it off we decorated it ourselves. It wasn't what I'd pictured my wedding to be but I tried to make the best of it.

We arrived to his sisters' house in his friends used limo. We walked into the house with our guests only to witness his cousin Lenny getting his hair pressed in the kitchen around all the food. The air reeked of hot grease, and burnt hair. I nearly lost my mind!

I was so embarrassed I ran out of the house into the backyard, straight into an eyesore. His sister had created this make shift back drop for people to take pictures in front of. It was constructed with a white sheet; Christmas lights, and garland wrapped around it, and it was hideous!

If I could have died, and gone to heaven at that very moment I would have. I just stood there before all my family, friends, and co-workers and cried.

I knew people were going to be laughing, and whispering behind my back, especially at work; because I would have done the same thing if I had been invited to a spectacle like this.

I grabbed the biggest bottle of Alcohol I could find, and tried to drown my sorrows. The more inebriated I became the less I cared about this hot mess of a wedding reception. I realized Rodney did the best he could and that's all that mattered to me.

We couldn't make ends meet with my income, and the little money Rodney was earning at the restaurant, so I created a resume for Rodney, and called a friend who gave him a job driving forklifts in a warehouse. A few months later we moved into a beautiful new four bedroom house.

Things in my life couldn't be better. I was happy, and content. I found myself head over heels for my new husband. I thought I'd finally found Mr. Right.

I helped him build his credit, and I co-signed for the new Cadillac that he always dreamed of. I was embarrassed to see my husband driving around in that rusty old car with primer on the front. I took him shopping, and got him a new wardrobe because I couldn't stand those cheap swap meet clothes he wore. I brought us both cell phones so we could communicate when we were apart.

Rodney handled the bills, and each month he would just tell me how much to pay, and I'd give him half of the money. I didn't use my phone much because I was at work most of the day, and at night I was home with my family.

One day Rodney told me my half of the bill was a hundred dollars. I couldn't believe the bill was so high because I barely used the phone, so I questioned him about it. I asked him to let me see the bill because I knew something was wrong. He handed me a partial bill with pages that were missing. When I brought it to his attention he proclaimed that was all the pages the cell phone company sent.

The next day I went to work, and happen to mention it to my carpool partner. She told me to go online, and set up an account so I could see the entire bill. When I pulled up the bill I was shocked. My portion of the bill was only thirty dollars. I couldn't believe Rodney had lied to me.

I printed the entire bill, and on the way home I began to study it. I noticed there were two phone numbers called consecutively at various times during the day and night.

I called the first number, and I reached a voicemail. The voice on the other end was a female who identified herself as Peanut. I called the second number, and it was a business. A women answered; and identified herself as Elizabeth. I told her my name, and inquired if there was anyone working there by the name of Peanut. She became silent then said that was her nickname.

I asked her why her number was on my husband's phone bill numerous times. She quickly asked "who's your husband?" and when I replied; "Rodney" she shut down. I continued saying hello until she finally responded. She said they worked together, and that they had been seeing each other for six months. She said Rodney told her he was divorced. I was in such amazement at what I had just heard that I just hung up the phone.

When I got home Rodney was upstairs lying in bed watching television. I had so much rage inside me. I couldn't believe he was cheating on me after everything I'd done for him. When I opened the bedroom door he greeted me with a smile, and before I knew it, I began throwing anything I could get my hands on.

He tried to duck, and jumped out of bed, and ran towards me to try to stop me. He grabbed me, and we both fell to the floor. He climbed on top of me, pinning my hands over my head. He asked me to calm down, and talk to him. I looked in his eyes and said "Who's Peanut?" His eyes got so big I thought they were going to pop out of his head. For a moment he didn't say anything, so I kept asking him over and over.

He grudgingly told me she was a girl he knew at work. He claimed they were merely friends, and nothing more. I asked him why he told her he was divorced if they were only friends. He claimed he told her he was married, and that she was lying. I could tell he was the one lying, but I played along like I was buying what he was selling. I convinced him to get off me, and that I was fine.

After a few minutes he slowly lifted me off the floor, and we both sat on the end of the bed. I whipped out the phone bill, and displayed the fourteen pages of phone calls he had, and compared it to the one page of phone calls I had. I questioned him on why he was calling Peanut all times of the day, and night. What could he have to talk about so important that it required him to call her constantly?

He pretended to be dumbfounded. I went downstairs, to make me a drink and I sat there alone thinking to myself "I got played again". It was now after midnight, and Rodney finally came downstairs to check on me. By then I had drank several shots of Tequila, and my mind was racing.

I slide open the patio door, and staggered into the back yard where he kept his weight bench. I picked up the long steel bar, and ran into the house, and started hitting him with it. He ran to the front door, and out of the house, but I was close behind.

I chased him, up and down the block until someone called the police. Our children were looking at us through the window when the police arrive. I was instructed to drop the weapon, and lay on the ground. I could see the fear in my son's eyes, because he'd never seen this side of me before. Rodney didn't press charges so the police let me go.

The next few weeks were difficult. I was heartbroken and I no longer trusted Rodney. The stress and anxiety caused my blood pressure to escalate and I suffered a heart attack at the age of forty.

My blood pressure was so high the doctors thought I was a sure candidate for a stroke. I was admitted into the intensive care unit at Loma Linda Medical center where I stayed for a week. When I came home Rodney was as sweet as candy and took good care of me.

He had planned a vacation to Las Vegas with some friends of his to try to work on our marriage. The day we were to depart I received a phone call from my sister Lisa. She told me that Mia was taken to the emergency room because she wasn't eating and complained of stomach pain.

Mia was always quiet; very secretive, and never complained. It was like pulling teeth just to get her to tell you anything. I told Rodney I wanted to go to the hospital to check on her before we left.

When we arrived to the hospital the doctor informed us that they were going to keep her overnight for observation, and to run a few tests.

When I walked into the hospital room, I saw Mia sitting up in bed, she looked up at me with this sad expression on her face; the whites of her eyes were yellow, and her stomach was swollen the size of a large watermelon.

My heart started beating fast, I knew it was something very serious. I remembered how little mama looked before she died and the thought brought me to tears.

I sat down beside her, and hugged her as tight as I could. Mia, and

I hadn't spoken or seen each other since Rodney, and I got married. She stopped speaking to me because I didn't ask her to be in my wedding.

Mia loved to drink and every time I saw her she was drunk. I was afraid she would embarrass me by being drunk so I didn't ask her to be in my wedding. She was so hurt that she didn't even come!

I sat next to her in the hospital bed, and from her appearance things didn't look good. I felt so guilty that I'd hurt my sister. I told her that when she got out of the hospital we'd go to Alcoholic Anonymous, and that we would both stop drinking. She looked at me, and in her slow soft spoken voice she said "Ok Rob". I started to cry so hard that my body started to shake all over. Mia hugged me, and said "Don't cry everything's gonna be alright".

I didn't want to leave her, but my family told me to go. The next day I received a call from my Lisa urging me to come home as soon as possible. She said Mia wasn't doing well. She had slipped into a coma, and was in intensive care.

I was devastated. Everything happened so fast. Is was just twenty-four hours that I had talked to her, now she was in a coma and her internal organs had started to shut down one by one. She was on Dialysis, and given blood transfusions.

My little sister was suffering, and there was nothing I could do to help her. Mia was in a coma ten days. I made a point not to miss a day at the hospital and even though she was in a coma I knew she could hear me so I talked to her about all the things we were going to do when she got better.

I was awaken suddenly from a deep drunken sleep on July thirty-first, two-thousand-two. I heard a voice in my head telling me to go see Mia. I jumped up, threw on some clothes, and drove to the hospital.

When I walked into Mia's room, I could see her chest moving up, and down so fast it looked as though she was fighting for air. She was breathing so hard and fast, her chest looked as though someone was beating drums.

I called mama and daddy from her hospital room and much to my surprise, no one answered. I ran around the hospital to find a doctor and bumped into a nurse who nonchalantly told me there is nothing they could do.

I left the hospital racing and running lights trying to get my parents. I beat on the door like the police and when mama answered, she looked at me and said "My baby's' dying, huh? " I looked at her, and told her to get to the hospital as fast as possible, then I drove home as fast as I could to get Michael.

Daddy, Mama, my sister Tina and my cousin Patricia went to the hospital. Mama said when she walked into room she could see Mia fighting to stay alive. Mama walked over to the left side of the bed, and put her hand on Mia's stomach and began to pray.

She spoke to her in a somber angelic voice and said "Baby if you're tired, you can go, we understand." After ten days in a coma Mia opened her eyes; took the oxygen mask off of her face, sat upright in the bed, and looked around at everyone in the room without saying a word. She calmly laid back in the bed, took a deep breath and died!

I was so consumed with guilt, because I wasn't there to help Mia when she needed me the most. I'd let my pride separate us. I didn't know how bad the alcohol had taken control of her life. She was my best friend, and I'd failed her. I chose my vanity over my sister, and I hurt the one person in the world who I knew loved me unconditionally.

I couldn't forgive myself. I sank into a deep depression, I began to drink day in and night out. I wanted to die with my sister. I always thought I'd be the first to die because of the type of lifestyle I lived, but that wasn't in God's plan.

On August seventh two-thousand-two, just seven days after Mia took her last breath; her body was laid to rest. I had to prepare myself to do one of the hardest things I'd ever had to do in my life.

We were lead into the small church where her coffin stood before us surrounded by lilies and roses. I couldn't take my eyes off the casket. I felt like I was in a fog and all the voices around me were echoes.

I heard my name called in the distance, so I stood to my feet and walked toward the pulpit. This wasn't like writing a speech, this was real and one of the hardest stories I had to tell. I read my sister's eulogy, and said goodbye to someone I sincerely loved and who truly loved me.

When Mia died part of me died with her. I was grateful because she left me a gift, her only son Warren, who was born on my birthday. I knew my life would never be the same again.

Rodney stood by my side when Mia died. He was bending over backwards trying to prove he loved me after I caught him cheating. He'd changed his cell phone number, and promised he wouldn't have any more female friends that I didn't know about.

The damage was done, the seed of deceit was planted, and his betrayal was embedded in my mind. My marriage was on the rocks, because I didn't trust Rodney anymore and the picture-perfect life I thought I was living was all a mirage.

I remembered when he was just a cook; driving around in that beat up old bucket, living in a roach infested apartment. Nobody wanted him but me.

I realized I'd cleaned and dressed him up; helped him get a new car and credit to make him presentable for another woman. I was the reason he lived in a beautiful new home, and had a decent job, yet he forget about all the sacrifices I'd made.

After Peanut there was Rhonda, Meredith, and Shay, the list was endless. If they had met him two years ago they wouldn't have given him the time of day.

One summer day out of the blue a woman called my cell phone. She identified herself as Renee. She was straight forward and polite. She informed me that she had been sleeping with Rodney for eight months. She wanted to talk to me in person and informed me that she knew where we lived.

When she arrived I was surprised to see this enormous woman standing at my front door. She had to be at least six feet tall, and she had the biggest hands and feet I'd ever seen on a female. At first I thought she was a transvestite.

I couldn't imagine her and Rodney as a couple, because he was a midget compared to her. I respected the fact that she was women enough to come to me, unlike all the other home wreakers who knew he was married and still messed around with him. I welcomed her into the house I shared with Rodney, it wasn't a home to me anymore because it was built on lies.

We sat down in the family room filled with photographs of Rodney and me. I offered her a glass of wine. She told me she met Rodney at the liquor store. I can't say I was surprised because he was an alcoholic.

She said they went out a few times to the beach and the movies, but that most of the time they were at her house. She began to suspect something wasn't right because every time she asked him to come to his house he made up an excuse, so she followed him home one night.

Renee was quite the character. She wasn't an ugly woman at all. She was just a giant, everything on her body was huge. From her head to her feet. She told me she was going to put her size twelve shoe up Rodney's ass. I'd never met a women who wore a size twelve shoe, but I was willing to pay for a front row seat to that fight. I advised her to hide her car because if he saw it he wouldn't come home.

When Rodney got home he walked into the house, and the expression on his face was priceless. I sat there, and watched as this big foot, drunk, amazon curse him out.

I thought I had a filthy mouth, but she took the cake. When Renee was finished she shook my hand; grabbed her purse and left.

I'd reached the point in my marriage that I accepted the fact that Rodney was a serial cheater. What hurt me the most was the type of women he was cheating with? They were hood rats, women with no class. Every time he cheated I caught him, I didn't even have to look and after a while it started to get old.

My family was skeptical about us getting married to begin with, because they knew we hadn't known each other long enough. I kept trying to make the marriage work, because we had built so much together in such a short time. I stayed because I didn't want to prove my family right.

I spent many lonely nights wondering where Rodney was, and why he didn't love me after everything I'd done for him. Three years of Rodney's cheating had taken a toll on me, and I was ready to do something.

One night my cousin Patricia called, and asked me to go out. I never went anywhere except work, so I agreed to go just to get out of the house. We went to a neighborhood bar to have drinks, and mingle. It was pretty boring, but it beat staying at home wondering when or if Rodney was coming home.

After the club we went to breakfast. We sat and talked until three in the morning, and then I dropped her off at home. When I drove into the driveway, and opened the garage door I noticed Rodney's car was there. I went into the house, and into our bedroom. My son and Rodney's youngest son were in the family room playing video games

It was summer so I didn't mind them staying up late. I walked into the room, and heard Rodney snoring. I tiptoed into the walk in closet, and started to undress. I put on my pajamas, and crawled into bed.

My face hadn't hit the pillow good before Rodney jumped on top of me, and started yelling. His breath stunk of stale cigarettes, and alcohol. He asked me where I'd been, but before I could say anything he began to take off my clothes. I insisted that he stop, and that's when he started accusing me of being out with another man.

I thought to myself how ironic the cheater calling me a cheater. He pulled down my panties, and shoved his fingers inside me as though he was giving me a pelvic exam. Then he pulled them out, and smelled them. He forcibly tried to have sex with me, and when I refused he snapped!

He put his hands around my throat; and begin dragging me from the bed into the walk in closet, and then he turned into a monster.

He began violently beating me like I was a man. Rodney lifted weights, and his arm and hands were huge. He punched me in the stomach several times. He slapped and choked me, and every time I'd cry he'd say; "You better stop crying or I'm going to kill you!"

I'd never seen this side of Rodney before, his face was disfigured, his eyes were blood shot red, and his tone of voice was deep, and frightening. I tried not to cry, but the brutal beating he was putting on my body was too much for me to endure.

When he realized he couldn't shut me up, he took one of his

Robin D. Barnes

leather belts, and wrapped it around my throat, and pulled with so much force that I started to lose conscientiousness. I fell to the floor, and bumped my head against the wall.

The beating went on for a while, then suddenly I heard a knock at the door; and a man's voice say "Open the door it's the police".

Rodney looked at me with this piercing glare in his eyes, and whispered "You better not say anything!" he removed the belt from around my neck, and picked me up off the floor. He led me into the bedroom. His entire demeanor had changed, like Dr. Jekyll, and Mr. Hyde.

I sat on the edge of the bed in silence. I was in shock at what just happened, and I was numb. The two officer's walked in, and stood in front of me, they looked down at me and said "Ma'am are you alright?" I just nodded my head.

One of the officers picked up the broken lamp that had fell on the floor when Rodney drug me off the bed. Rodney started asking the cops why they were here, and they quickly told them us the children called because they heard a disturbance.

The officer advised us that the kids were so afraid that they were found hiding in the bushes. Rodney appeared to be shocked, and tried to talk his way out of it, but the officers weren't buying it. They knew I wasn't going to talk with Rodney standing there so they took him downstairs to question him.

The officer asked me to stand up, and walk into the bathroom into the light. I got up slowly; I could hardly move, every muscle, and bone in my body hurt.

He took one look at me, and his facial expression said it all. He told me to look in the mirror. I turned slowly, and the image before me was that of someone who had been in a boxing match.

My eyes were swollen; my lip were bleeding, and my neck looked as though someone had tried to lynch me. My clothes were torn, and my hair was a mess. Rodney beat me worse than Keith ever had.

The officer began taking pictures. He kept asking me what happened, but I kept remembering what Rodney had whispered in the closet, so I never said a word.

The officer tried to reassure me that they would protect me, but I still didn't say a word. I knew all too well that the police weren't going to protect me, and I was afraid of what Rodney would do to me if I told. What I didn't know, was that the kids told them enough. They told them that they heard me screaming, and crying for help.

Michael heard Rodney telling me to shut up or he was going to kill me! They handcuffed Rodney, and arrested him that night. I never saw this coming, in the three years we had been together Rodney had never displayed any type of anger or violence towards me.

He was too busy lying, and cheating on me and when he wasn't doing that; he was passed out drunk. Rodney knew my story; how I'd been physically abused in the past, and he promised he would never hurt me. He broke his promise to me like every other man had in the past, and now I was left with nothing but humiliation.

I couldn't go to work for a week, and I refused to leave my house, because I didn't want the neighbors or my family to see me. I just stayed in bed, and drank until I passed out. This went on for days. I just couldn't take it anymore. I couldn't understand why every man I loved only thought of me as a punching bag, and treated me as if my feelings didn't matter.

Rodney kept calling from jail, and for the first few days I wouldn't answer, then one day for some unknown reason I answered the phone. I don't know why, but I did.

The voice on the phone was far from the voice in the closet that night. It was Dr. Jekyll and he crying, telling me how sorry he was, and that he didn't know what came over him. He begged me to help him, and promised that he'd go to counseling, and anger management.

Rodney claimed he had blacked out and didn't remember anything that happened. He said he wanted to save our marriage, and was willing to do anything to demonstrate that to me. He sounded so convincing, or maybe I just wanted to believe that he meant what he was saying; so like a fool; I bailed him out.

When Rodney came home things started to change. He stopped hanging out in the streets, and he slowed down on the drinking. He started going to church with me every Sunday, and counseling twice a week with our pastor. He read the bible, and prayed every night before we went to bed.

It's funny how fear can make you run to God, and he was definitely afraid. He was facing his third strike, and the prosecutor wouldn't drop the case, even though I never admitted anything happened. My son's testimony, and the pictures of me that night were enough for them to prosecute him.

I gradually saw a difference in Rodney's behavior as the months progressed. I was sure that he had changed. I believed that our marriage had a chance to survive, so I persuaded Michael to change his testimony. He begged me not to make him do it; the look in his eyes were of disappointment, and confusion. Michael went on and on about how badly Rodney treated me; how he'd lied, and cheated on me numerous times.

He said he heard me crying for help when Rodney beat me. He couldn't understand why I wanted to help him, but I pleaded with him to just do it, and when the trial started Michael recanted his story to the prosecutor and the jury, against his will.

I testified that I started a fight with Rodney because I found out he was cheating. I convinced a jury that my son, and I were both liars; to save Rodney from going back to prison for the rest of his life.

I played the role of my life, and if there was an academy given for best idiot in a courtroom I would have won. I even had my pastor testify on Rodney's behalf, and he even wrote a character letter on his behalf.

Of course he wasn't aware that Rodney was really guilty and had done all the things he was being accused of. After eight hours of deliberation the jury found Rodney "not guilty".

It was a difficult moment for me because my son never looked at me the same. Rodney went to church that Sunday after the verdict, and stood in front of the entire congregation, and testified how God have spared his life. I was convinced I'd done the right thing by helping him, but I was wrong.

It wasn't a full thirty days before Rodney forgot all the promises he'd made to me, and God. He went back to his old ways; lying, cheating, and drinking.

He stopped going to church, and marriage counseling. I'd made the ultimate sacrifice for him; I ruined my relationship with my son, only to find out it was all a charade. Rodney played me, my son and the church. I was so hurt, and embarrassed; that I stopped attending church, because I couldn't face my pastor, or the congregation anymore!

My alcohol addiction was out of control again. I was drinking, and taking pills more than ever. The guilt I felt inside was tremendous. I'd hurt the one person in this world that I knew loved me; my son. Things between Michael, and I were strained. He started getting into trouble at school. He became disrespectful, and it was all my fault.

I destroyed my relationship with my son for a man that didn't give a damn about me. My son's entire attitude was altered. The once happy go lucky demeanor he had was gone. He started running away from home, smoking weed and drinking. He got involved in gangs and dropped out of high school all because of me. I had failed him.

I didn't know what to do to fix things, so I did the only thing I knew how to do, and that was to try to buy his love. I gave him anything he asked for; just to try to make him happy. I tried to fill the void that I caused in our relationship; with gifts, and money, and it seemed to work despite the fact that he lost all respect for me.

I'd finally had enough of Rodney's infidelity. The only thing we shared was the same last name, and address. We were sleeping in separate rooms; and scarcely speaking to each other.

I would pray for him to drink himself to death, or crash his car while he was drunk driving, so I could collect the life insurance money. I believed I deserved that much after all the years of bullshit I endured.

I tried to work as much overtime as possible just so I wouldn't have to go home. That's when I met Kendall. We worked for the same company, but in different departments. I would always see him standing alone on the phone in the smoking section during break and lunch. There was something about him that captured my attention.

Kendall wasn't fine like Keith, and he wasn't repugnant like Rodney. He had an air about himself that was attractive. He was tall; slim, with a short tapered haircut, and light brown eyes. He had a golden brown skin tone, with a dimple in his chin.

We struck up a conversation one day, and from that point on we were inseparable. We scheduled all our breaks at the same time just so we could talk.

Kendall was from New York and talked with an east coast accent. He'd moved to California after his wife died suddenly from an aneurism. He was left to raise three children alone.

Our relationship started off innocent with no strings attached. Kendall was a breath of fresh air. He was funny; thoughtful, and he made me laugh. He complimented me every time he saw me, and soon I labeled him, "my at work husband." We joked about it, and kept it strictly plutonic because Kendall was married.

Kendall had re-married a psychotic white women name Diana. He told me they'd only been married a few years, when he'd found out she was bipolar, and refused to take her medication. Her mood swings, and insecurity had affected their relationship tremendously.

Kendall didn't like the fact that his wife didn't try to get close to his children. He said she was nice, and loving towards them in the beginning of their relationship but after they married everything changed.

He'd claimed that he attempted to leave her a few times, but she'd threaten suicide, so he stayed with her out of pity and obligation. He shared his innermost thoughts, and feelings with me, and I shared my mine with him. We connected in a way Rodney, and I never had.

Kendall, and I had gotten so close that he introduced me to his children and ironically; we hit it off. I told Michael about Kendall, and he was happy that I'd found someone that really cared about me. He couldn't wait for me to divorce Rodney. For the first time in a long time things between Michael and I seemed to be getting better.

It was now the spring of 2005. I was still trapped in a loveless marriage. The only thing I was holding on to was a house and a few material things. Rodney had been promoted on his job to a trainer, which required him to travel. I really didn't care what he did, or where he went anymore, the less I saw of him the better. I loved when he was gone, because that meant I could spend more time with Kendall.

We had finally crossed the line in our relationship one night after work, when we met at a local bar with some other co-workers for drinks. One thing led to another, and on a dare; we kissed right in front of everyone.

We ended up in a hotel adjacent to our job, and we had the most passionate night of love making I'd ever had. It was sensual and seductive. I think I loved it because it was forbidden.

Kendall didn't rush, he pampered, and adore my body. He touched every inch of me, and made me feel like a real woman. I even came close to an orgasm, but for some unknown reason I couldn't quite get there. I think it was because the lights were on in the room, and I feared he would see my scares. I was still self-conscience about my body after all these years. I couldn't relax long enough to put down my guard. Kendall was a caring lover who took his time to please me. We found comfort in each other, and I knew there was no going back.

When Rodney told me that he had to go to Chicago for a month; I was ecstatic. I couldn't wait to drop him off at the airport. The plane hadn't left the runway before I called Kendall. He brought his daughters, and grand-daughter, and they stayed at the house with me, and my son for the entire month that Rodney was gone.

We all got along, and enjoyed each other's company. His daughter were a few years older than Michael, and they treated him like their little brother. As dysfunctional as it may have been, we were all happy. I loved his children, and they loved me. Michael admired, and respected Kendall because he made me happy.

Two years went by quickly, and it was now 2007. Kendall, and I were still hot, and heavy in our love triangles. Rodney was so busy sneaking around thinking he was cheating on me, that he didn't have a clue what I was doing.

I'd fallen madly in love with Kendall and I wanted out of my marriage. We'd talked about divorcing our insignificant others several times, but Kendall had a soft spot for his wife's mental issues. I didn't want him to leave his wife to be with me, but I did think he should leave his wife for his children. She didn't even want his kids to stay in their house.

His wife didn't try to have a relationship with them because she was jealous, and controlling. She had a problem with most black females according to Kendall, I think she was just intimidated because she wanted to be black. She had a half black son from a previous relationship, and had only been involved with black men.

I arrived to work at five am Monday morning. I was in a good mood, because Kendall, and I had spent the weekend together. I sat down at my desk, and noticed that the red light on my phone was blinking, which meant I had messages. I put my phone on speaker, so that I could write down the information if needed, and what I heard blew my mind. I had fifty messages, and they were all from Kendall's wife!

Before I could take the phone off speaker the first thing I heard was; "Raven, you Bitch", and then she kept saying the same thing repeatedly, while threatening what she was going to do to me. I couldn't believe what I was hearing.

She called the receptionist, and human resources department, and informed them that I was sleeping with her husband, and that I was a home wrecker. My manager overheard the threats of violence, and called the police.

I called Kendall's office, and reached his voicemail. I called his cell phone, and got no answer. I was really worried that she'd killed him, or that something bad had happened.

The police arrived, and listened to all the messages. They considered them terrorist threats, and filed a police report. They advised me to get a restraining order as soon as possible.

My job hired private security to come to the job to ensure my safety, because they deemed her as a threat. I was escorted to the bathroom, to lunch, and to my car.

A few days passed, and I still hadn't heard from Kendall, and he hadn't been back to work. I called his daughters, and was told that his wife tried to commit suicide and that Kendall was out on disability.

She'd purposely set the house on fire with herself, and the dog inside, but not before she spray painted that I was a whore, and Kendall was a cheater in big bold black spray paint on the front of their brick fence. She went as far as printing flyers; putting them on all the neighbors' cars telling them about our affair.

Kendall was accurate by saying she was crazy, and so was he for dealing with it! I knew my relationship with Kendall was over. He'd taken a leave of absence from work to try to help his wife; who was admitted into a mental hospital.

Six months went by and I didn't hear or see Kendall. I knew that he wasn't going to leave his wife now because of her mental illness, and because he was just too kind hearted.

I had to let go of Kendall as much as it hurt, because I knew what I was doing was wrong. He came back to work after several months and he attempted to avoid me, and I tried to do the same but we just couldn't leave each other alone and before long we were sneaking around with each other again.

Kendall played this back, and forth game between me, and his wife for four years. It had gotten to the point that his wife would call me, and personally ask me to leave her husband alone. She would call me all kinds of black bitches, and make threats, and I'd laugh, and torture her by telling her; she wished she was black.

This went on for years, and I must confess I was getting tired of it. One day out of the clear blue, Kendall called me, and asked me to meet him. When I pulled up I noticed his black Infinity had dents all over it. His windshield was cracked, and his backseat was full of clothes. He told me he'd left his wife for good! He said that he had enough, and that he was getting a divorce. He asked me to move in with him, and without so much as a thought; I agreed. I thought I'd finally won the prize. We spent the night together making plans for our future.

When I arrived home that Sunday morning; I was in high spirits, until I saw Rodney's car in the garage. When I walked in he was sitting in his usual chair drinking a beer; watching football.

I walked in with my over-night bag; without saying a word, I went into the bathroom to take a shower. When I came out, Rodney had the audacity to ask me where I'd been. I thought this was rather strange, since we barely spoke when we did see each other.

I sat on the bed, and blurted out," I was with my boyfriend; his name is Kendall, we've been together for four years, we're in love, and I want a divorce."

I said this without so much as taking one breathe! Rodney looked at me, his eyes expanded, and his mouth fell open, but nothing came out, it was if someone hit the mute button. I thought he was going to hit me, but I was prepared this time, because I kept a knife underneath my pillow every night just in case he tried something.

Without warning Rodney begin sobbing like a baby. It didn't move me one bit, because I thought it was just an act so I sat there for a few minutes waiting for him to snap, but he didn't.

Instead he got up, grabbed his keys, and left. I got in the bed, and went to sleep. That was the best night's sleep I'd ever had. I was awakened around two o' clock in the morning by Rodney, he claimed he wasn't feeling well. He said that his head, and chest hurt. I thought it was just a desperate attempt at seeing if I cared, so I gave him some Tylenol, and went back to sleep.

An hour later he awakened me again, he was starting to irritate me by now with his whining and crying. This time he couldn't breathe, and his chest hurt. He was begging me to take him to the hospital. All the while I was thinking to myself "Hurry up and die" then I told him to call one of his girlfriends to take him to the hospital. I had no compassion for him whatsoever, and I wasn't falling for anymore of his exploits. I thought it was just another ploy for attention until he started vomiting profusely all over the bathroom floor. I reluctantly got dressed, and drove him to the emergency room.

At first I was going to be a heartless bitch, and just drop him off and leave. Then I felt like it would be cold-blooded of me to just leave him there on the curb like and unwanted dog, even though he would have done that to me.

I wasn't a callous person, void of mercy until Rodney broke my heart, and demolished my trust. As soon as we got in the emergency room he was rushed into observation, and they performed an EKG.

The doctor notified me that Rodney was having a heart attack, and that he had several of them before we came. He needed emergency surgery immediately. The strange thing was I felt nothing, I still thought it was an act, and that I was being played.

Rodney had done so much to me that I couldn't feel any emotion towards him anymore. I called his children, and they met me at the hospital. Once they arrived I went home to get Rodney's medical insurance, and his cell phone so I could contact his job.

It was six am Monday morning I figured Kendall would be headed for work so I called him to tell him what was happening, but I got no answer.

When I got home I searched our bedroom looking for Rodney's phone. He made it his life's mission to always hide it from me, but no matter where he buried it, God would always lead me to it. Once he tried a James Bond maneuver, and concealed it under his car seat with Velcro, but I found it.

This time I located it hidden in the back of the walk-in closet in a stack of sweaters. As soon as I turned it on I could see he had several text messages from someone named M.D. Rodney would always use initials or code name so I wouldn't know they were females. I was Ms. X on his phone.

The messages read "where are you baby?" I responded by telling her to call me, and when she did I told her that he had a heart attack, and was in the hospital.

She told me her name which didn't matter to me, and asked why I had his phone. She then announced that she was his girlfriend. Seems they'd been together six months. I laughed, and told her I was his wife, she seemed surprised, but I wasn't. I told her where she could find him, and ended the call. As far as I was concerned my marriage was over, and I was going to be with the man I loved; so whatever Rodney was doing didn't matter to me any longer.

After five hours; the surgery was over, and Rodney was moved into intensive care. I hadn't talked to Kendall since he'd told me he was leaving his wife. I wasn't sure what to think this time, but whatever happened wouldn't be a surprise.

I went to work a few days later, and I still hadn't heard from Kendall, so I went to his office. His supervisor told me he hadn't been to work since Friday.

A week had come, and gone and still no word from Kendall. I called his friend Danny, who Kendall told me he'd be staying with until we got a place. Danny was hesitant to say anything at first, then he regretfully told me that Kendall went back to his wife.

A sense of guilt came over me, and I started to feel like I was to blame for Rodney's heart attack. Kendall had taken me on that emotional rollercoaster ride once again, and I felt like a fool for having faith in him, considering all the times he'd lied in the past. Now I felt obligated to stay with Rodney, and I'd made up my mind that I was finished with Kendall for good.

Rodney came home from the hospital two weeks later, and we tried to make it work. After all the cheating he'd done to me; he had the audacity to be hurt because I cheated on him. I couldn't understand why he could cheat, and it was alright, but when I cheated I was a whore?

Rodney got a taste of his own medicine, and he didn't like the flavor. He tried to justify it by saying he never loved any of the numerous floozies he cheated on me with, but in my eyes he never loved me.

He jeopardized our marriage just to gratify himself. He tried to tell me he had a sex addiction, so I told him to add that to the list of other addictions that he had, which were alcohol, drugs, cheating, and lying.

I'd finally reached the point that I didn't care about anyone's feelings, but my own. I didn't filter my words; I didn't walk around on egg shells trying to please him, and I didn't pretend with Rodney anymore. He knew what I was capable of now. I had a four year affair right under his nose, and I had mastered the art of cheating.

I had a separate cell phone that Rodney knew nothing about, and I didn't mess around with the next door neighbor. Rodney was sloppy, he always found women that lived in our neighborhood to cheat with, and he always got caught.

Rodney, and I agreed to give our dysfunctional relationship one more try. After all we'd been married for over seven years and most of it was hell. I only agreed to it because I knew it was over with Kendall, and I had nothing to lose.

After Rodney recovered from his surgery I decided to end the marriage. I packed up his belongings and when he came home from the hospital the locks were changed. He tried to plead with me to try to work it out, but it was over and had been over the very first time he lied, cheated and abused me.

I didn't want to waste another minute of my life in a fraudulent marriage. It wasn't about Kendall or anyone else. It was about me, and what I stood for. I'd reduced myself to the same kind of slut that was cheating with my husband. How could I be blessed sleeping with another woman's man? If he did it to her he would do it to me. It was time for me to move on by myself and stop depending on a nothing ass man to take me where I wanted to go.

A few months went by and I moved out of the house into an apartment. I couldn't afford the mortgage payment and the house went into foreclosure. I was starting fresh and I had peace for the first time in a long time.

I didn't have to worry about no sorry man barking demands at me or wanting to have sex with me when I wasn't in the mood. I didn't have to cook and clean up after anyone else but myself, and I didn't have to worry about anyone lying, cheating or putting their hands on me ever again, because I was free and I wasn't afraid of being alone anymore.

I found out a few months later that Rodney had gotten a twenty-five year old girl pregnant, maybe that's what caused his heart attack. I know if I got pregnant at forty-six I'd have a heart attack and probably drop dead. I felt sorry for the child. She found my number in Rodney's phone and wanted to meet me. I couldn't understand for the life of me why but I agreed. We met at Applebee's one Friday afternoon. She introduced herself and reached out her hand to shake mine.

We walked into the restaurant, and were seated. I didn't say a word for a few minutes, because I wanted to hear what she had to say. She told me that they'd been together for over a year, and she was five months pregnant.

She said that Rodney told her he was divorced. I still didn't say a word because I was still trying to wrap my mind around the fact that this child was sitting in front of me telling me she is pregnant by my forty-six year old husband.

She said that she knew something was wrong, because he wouldn't tell her where he lived. She went on to say that Rodney came over to her house and after having sex with her he fell asleep. She went through his phone, and saw a text message from me. She wrote down the number, but didn't call right away because she didn't know how I'd react. I was blown away.

All this time I was thinking I was the cause of his heart attack, and now I find out it was because he was stressed out because he'd gotten someone's child knocked up!

I looked into the face of this young child; with her fake eyelashes, blue contacts, long cheap synthetic weave, and braces and I felt sorry for her.

I reached over, and held her hand. I told her how sad I was that she'd been taken advantage of. She started to cry so hard I could see her body tremble. She said this was her first baby and that she was in nursing school, and had been introduced to Rodney by a friend.

She said he told her he was thirty-five. My mouth nearly hit the floor! How in the hell could she believe he was in his thirties with all that gray hair? Not to mention he looked old.

Then I remembered Rodney had started dying his hair and his mustache, but other parts of his body were still gray.

She said that she didn't want to cause any problems, and that when she told Rodney she was pregnant; he denied being the father, and told her he had a vasectomy.

I didn't know what else to say to console the poor girl. When I told her how old Rodney was, she said he was the same age as her father.

We ordered dinner; ate, and left the restaurant. I thanked her for having the guts to call me, and for being such a respectful young lady.

She told me how beautiful I was, and wondered why Rodney would ever cheat on me. I simply told her; "his penis doesn't have eyes, and he doesn't have a conscience." I informed her that she wasn't the first women he cheated on me with, but she was the last! That was the end of my marriage to Rodney.

Chapter Twenty-One

Looking for Love in All the Wrong Places

I'd wasted so many years of my life searching for someone to love me. Fantasizing that one day he'd ride up on his big white horse, and rescue me; just like in all the fairy tales. I wanted to live happily ever after, but all I found were the liars, cheaters, womanizers and abusers.

I wasn't specific in my request to God about what kind of man I wanted. I just prayed that God would send me a man, and that's just what I got. I had every type of man from the mama's boy to the closet bisexual.

I didn't know I needed to be detailed in my description of the type of man I wanted. So instead of finding a man of substance with morals, and values who appreciated a woman's worth, and knew how to love; I constantly conjured up the wrong type of man.

I was broken and I kept attracting men that were broken too. I thought I could save them, but all the while I was the one who needed to be saved.

Most of them were opportunist who preyed on my weaknesses. I thought I had to have a man to acknowledge my being, and give me self-worth, but none of them did that.

All they did was take what they could, and run. I didn't think I was good enough to require anything from them, because my life held no value to me.

In my mind the person I saw in the mirror with eyes just like mine was a shell with a painted face, and a fake smile. My soul cried out for someone to love me, someone to care about what I thought, and how I felt.

I was too afraid to tell them what I needed; so my mouth stayed shut, and my mask stayed on. I pretended to be happy with whatever they were willing to give; which consisted of hurt and pain most of the time.

Almost every intimate relationship I had ended in disaster, because I wasn't being real with myself or with them. I kept making the same poor choices in men, because I didn't love me.

All of them saw my insecurities, and used them to manipulate me. None of them recognized me as a women with feelings, because I didn't make them understand that my feelings mattered. I saw them as a means to an end, and they saw me as an opportunity to come up.

I took care of every man I'd ever been involved with. I never demanded they do anything for me, because I was too afraid they would leave me.

I bent over backwards, and took whatever I had to take off of them just to have someone in my life. The sad thing is; no matter what I did it was never good enough.

I was so afraid of rejection that I settled for whatever a man did to me even if it was cheating or physically abusing me, because being alone with myself, and my thoughts were worst then that.

Nobody I let into my world was who they said they were, but I was still willing to accept their lies, because I was living a lie too. How could I expect them to be honest with me, when I wasn't being honest myself?

I'd lied, and pretended so long; that I lost sight of who I was, and what I deserved. The world I created was a place I learned to accept, because there I didn't feel like a failure.

In my world I could hide from myself, and become someone else, and that's just what I did. In my quest for Mr. Right; I encountered Several Mr. Right now's, and Mr. Wrongs.

Rodney was a lesson, he along with every other man that had come, and gone in my life taught me something about myself. I blamed them for not loving, and respecting me, when I didn't love or respect myself. They treated me like I treated myself, because I gave them permission to.

I realized I wasn't the victim, I was the perpetrator. I never specified the type of man I wanted, and I didn't have a checklist of the requirements a man needed to have to be with me.

I accepted whomever exhibited the least bit of interest in me. It didn't matter what they had to offer; as long as they showed me a little attention, and they needed me.

I was like a chameleon, and changed who I was every time I was with a man, just to satisfy his ego. None of them loved me; they used me to better their situation.

When they got what he needed from me; I was no longer relevant or necessary. I built them up and they beat me down. I allowed them to do the things they did to me, because I had no belief in myself that I deserved better.

When I finally decided enough was enough it didn't hurt anymore, and when I finally opened my eyes, and saw the part I played in the game of life I knew I had no one else to blame but myself.

I'd come to the conclusion that maybe I needed to stop looking for love. Stop relying on anyone; man or women to make me happy, and just be satisfied with being with myself.

It was too much work trying to have a relationship. Trusting someone with my heart; only to get it broken time, and time again had taken its toll on me.

So I gave up my search for Mr. Right, and began to focus on the things that I had control of; which was finding out who I was, and getting my life pointed in the right direction.

I must admit deep inside I was lonely, but I was alone when I was married, and I was by myself when I was in my so called relationships.

Two years had passed since I left Rodney and the only regret I had was staying as long as I did. I don't know how I expected a relationship built on sand to have a solid foundation. It was a marriage of convenience and I was glad it was finally over.

I had engulfed myself in my new business. I was grossing twenty thousand dollars a month, so it was easy for me to forget about love, because I had money.

I was doing just fine without a man, or at least that's what I was telling myself. I had my trusty vibrator and it never let me down. It didn't lie, complain, abuse or cheat on me. It only gave out when it needed new batteries and I didn't have to listen to it snore or smell it fart. I didn't have to cook for it or worry about it seeing me naked.

All I had to do was turn it on, make myself feel good and turn it off when I'd had enough.

I wish they made men with an on and off switch, a remote control that could pause and put them on mute; then I could have the perfect man. Until then I guess it's just me and "BOB" my "Battery Operated Boyfriend".

Chapter Twenty-Two

Mr. Right Found Me

It was in the fall of 2010, when I met him. This tall, dark handsome southern gentleman from Texas with his clean shaven head, chocolate colored skin, dimples, and alluring smile. He stood about six feet four, and spoke with a southern accent that knocked me off my feet.

My friends always told me that Mr. Right would find me; but I was always too anxious, and never waited long enough for that to happen.

I had taken my girlfriend Stacy to a jazz club to get her mind off losing her husband. He'd just passed away a few months prior from cancer at the age of forty-one. I was with her the day he died in their bedroom. It was a surreal moment that I will never forget. It really made me appreciate life a lot more.

Stacy was grieving, and I wanted to help her as much as I could so I thought getting her out of the house would do her some good.

I called around, and found a local jazz spot. I thought it would be nice for us to just relax, listen to some music, and have a few drinks. A change of scenery would make us both feel much better.

We stepped into the dimly lit club, and searched for a table. The place was intimate, and there weren't many people there yet, and I liked that because I didn't like crowds. Stacy and I found a table right in front of the band and the dance floor.

I liked the atmosphere; it had a good vibe. Everyone looked to be thirty, and over; which was something else I liked. I never liked mingling with kids, and it seemed like that's all I attracted.

I'd never been with a man my age, because I was blessed to look young for my age, so the tiny boppers always tried to hit on me.

Don't get me wrong I am a cougar, I didn't want nothing old but money, but I still knew where to draw the line.

The youngest man I'd ever dated was nineteen, and I was thirty. It was a hot mess, he got sprung, and became a stalker. One day he came to my job and ransacked the office looking for me, because I told him it was over. After I lost that job I vowed to never date a man who was not old enough to buy liquor again.

Stacy and I ordered drinks, and appetizers while we waited for the band to perform. I glanced around the room looking for potential targets, but I didn't see anyone I would remotely be interested in, but it was still early.

I got up to take a walk to the bathroom. When I came back, I noticed the club had begun to fill up. I hurried back to my seat, and just as I started to sit down; someone from behind whispered "Let me get that for you" and he pulled out my chair.

As I turned to thank him, I found my eyes planted right in his chest. I slowly lifted my head to gain eye contact, and there he was; prince charming.

I tried to remain nonchalant, so as not to appear desperate, or nervous. I calmly said "thank you" and sat down. He introduced himself as Ramon, and held his hand out to shake mine. When I put my hand into his; I could feel an energy like I'd never felt before.

It was as if someone plugged me into a light socket, and a surge of energy shot through my entire body! It was a feeling I'd never felt before. I could feel butterflies forming in my stomach, and I was at a loss for words. Ramon continued the conversation by asking me if I'd ever been there before.

I felt like a teenager at the high school dance at that moment, and before I knew it, he invited himself to sit down. For the rest of the night Ramon and I talked, laughed, and danced.

He told me he was from Texas, and that he was only here for the night. When it was time to leave; he grabbed my hand, and walked me to my car as though we were a couple. We exchanged numbers, and said goodbye. I thought that was the end of that, because Ramon lived thousands of miles away, and I knew our paths would probably never cross again.

As it turns out Ramon was a long distance truck driver, and traveled constantly across the country. We talked to each other three or four times a day every day after we met. It was refreshing to talk to a man who had morals, and values. Who was educated; articulate, a good father, and a hard worker.

He had dreams, and goals; wanted something out of life for himself, and his children. He had a five year plan, and he knew what he wanted in a women.

The most important thing I loved and admired about Ramon; was that he loved God. He spent a lot of time in church, and although he was on the road ninety percent of the time; he always found a way to get in to some church whenever he was.

Ramon was separated when we met, and I just couldn't believe someone let this good man slip away. I always believed someone's trash is someone else's treasure and I wasn't going to look a gift horse in the mouth.

A little over a month had passed since I met Ramon. Although all we had was a long distance relationship it was more meaningful to me than any relationship I'd had in my life, because I could be myself.

Ramon called to let me know he'd be in California for a couple of days, and he wanted to see me. I couldn't wait to see him again. I dreamed about him every night and would fall asleep on the phone with him because I didn't want to hang up.

When he arrived at the truck stop in Ontario, California he called me to pick him up. When I got there my heart was fluttering, and my hands were shaking. I felt like a school girl going on a first date.

When I saw him walking towards my car it took my breath away. He looked even better the second time, and when he reached my car; I got out to greet him.

He dropped his bags, and wrapped his big strong arms around my waist; bent down, and gave me the most passionate kiss I'd ever had. We stood there in the parking lot for what seemed to be hours, but was actually only a few minutes, just hugging, and kissing like two teenagers in love.

When Ramon, and I arrived to my house, it was as if we'd been together for a lifetime. We cooked dinner together; had a drink, listened to some music, and talked.

I'd never talked to a man like I could talk to Ramon. I could tell him anything; he would just listen, and once I finished he'd give me his opinion. He was never judgmental about anything I said. He let me have an opinion; which was something I wasn't accustomed to with other men.

I thought to myself "This was turning out to be one of the best nights of my life." I couldn't wait to get him into bed, and rock his world, but Ramon took his time. He didn't rush to do anything, because he respected me.

He grabbed his bag, and went into the bathroom to take a shower. I'd never known a man to take a shower that long before. He was in that bathroom for over an hour. I put two and two together and came to the conclusion that he was preparing himself for me.

When he walked out of the bathroom there I was lying across my bed in my Victoria Secret black lace Lingerie, with six inch stilettos'. The candles were lit and placed in various parts of the room, while Luther Vandross was softly playing in the distance.

I stood up, and performed a slow sexy dance for him. When I was finished he positioned me on the bed face down and slowing began to massage hot oil on my feet and legs.

When here reached my butt he began to remove my thong and then he tried to undress me. I still hadn't overcome that scar on my stomach so I stopped him by taking over.

I laid him down and began massaging him from head to toe. I blew out the candles so the room could be pitch black, and he couldn't see my naked body. I took off my clothes and crawled on top of him and rubbed my hot oily body on his.

He wrapped his big muscular arms around me and I could feel the passion that I'd always longed for. It wasn't like the normal sexual encounters I was use too. It was two people totally into each other. He cared about how I felt, and what I liked. He took his time to make sure I was pleased, and he didn't try to destroy my body like all the others. It was passionate, and personal. Every inch of my body was treated with respect.

I'd never been treated in this manner before, and I didn't know how to react to such pleasure. So I laid there, and cried silently and enjoyed the moment. I heard a soft voice whisper in my ear as I experienced my very first orgasm with a man. The voice said; "He's the one."

It scared me so bad I started to shiver. I don't know if it was from the immense pleasure that encompassed my body, or just fear, but Ramon stopped in mid-stroke; looked into my eyes, and asked me if I was ok. I just nodded my head up and down like a puppet; to gesture yes because I was unable to speak.

We made love until the sun came up, and from that night on I knew what loving, and caring about someone really felt like. Ramon showed me how a man was supposed to make love to a women. He made me feel relevant; like I meant something, and I was somebody special. Each, and every time I saw him I began to feel worthy of his love.

Our relationship blossomed into something I'd never imagined. And for the first time in my life, I'd met someone who didn't want anything from me, but my love. At the age of forty-seven I encountered someone who finally loved, and adored me; for me.

Ramon wasn't just my lover; he was my best friend. I loved that he was interested in what I thought, and how I felt. My dreams mattered to him, and his mattered to me. A year and a half had passed, and Ramon and I were going strong.

I knew Ramon was tired of being on the road. He despised be- ing away from his mother who was ill and his children. He confided in me that he wanted to stop driving trucks, and open his own business.

Ramon was very intelligent, he'd graduated from Texas University with honors. He achieved his bachelor's degree in communication and was working on his masters' degree.

Ramon adored his children, and that was one of many reasons I loved him so much. I only wished my children had a father like him. No matter where he was; if one of his children called, and needed something, he'd make sure they got it.

Finally the day arrived, and he told me he wouldn't be driving trucks to California anymore. He'd found a job in Texas driving locally.

I knew how much it meant to him to be in his children's life, but I was still heartbroken that I wouldn't see him again. He asked me to come to Texas. I really wanted to be with him; but I was afraid. I'd up rooted myself several times in the past for a man. I'd left everything I had; including my kids only to regret it in the end. I had promised myself I would never do that again.

I pondered the thought of relocating for months, and every time I tried to get the courage to do it; I'd think about my children who were now adults; with families of their own.

I had five grandchildren who loved, and adored me. I was finally in a good place with my family, and I couldn't jeopardize what took me so long to build, for the promises of a man.

I made the decision to stay in California. I thought it would be selfish of me to leave. I spent so much of my life running from man to man looking for love; always putting my children on the back burner, because I was thinking only of myself.

I thought what if I get there, and he changes just like all the others had? What if I give up everything again, only to end up with nothing?

The fear overwhelmed me, and I became consumed with guilt over all the time I had wasted looking for love in all the wrong places.

I wanted Ramon so badly, but at what cost? I wanted that feeling of love, and security that he gave me, but I was scared to take another chance at love; so love left me behind, and I was alone again!

A year had passed; Ramon, and I would talk on the phone from time to time; sharing tidbits of our lives. I stopped calling him because it hurt too bad to hear his voice. I knew I had given up the love of my life; yet there was nothing I could do.

I tried to get over Ramon by meeting other people, but no one came close to him. He was "the one" and I knew it. The one good man who'd ever walked into in my life; and I had to let him go. I often wondered what if I had taken that leap of faith just one more time.

What if Ramon was my last chance at real; unconditional love? I just let him walk away without a fight. I always knew I loved hard, and that most of the men in my life didn't deserve, or appreciate me but Ramon did.

I begin to understand that my love wasn't meant for everyone, and that God sent the one man for me to love that was equally yoked.

I learned the power of love. I began to love myself more and more. I knew I couldn't be anything to anyone until I was something to myself. I accepted that maybe I might end up alone, and I'm ok with that now. I'm not afraid or ashamed of who I am anymore. I'm proud of the woman I've become.

I'm blessed to be here to repair the broken pieces of my life. I'm thankful to Ramon for sharing that experience with me. An emotion as extraordinary as real love may only come once in a lifetime. Even if that was my last chance at love; at least I had it once, and it's better to have been loved once then to never have loved at all.

Ramon moved on with his life, and every so often we still talk. I know he truly loved me, so it makes it easier to accept that he's gone. He chose me. For once in my life someone chose to love me, and that felt good.

I didn't have to work for his love. I didn't have to pretend for his acceptance. I didn't have to lie, or become someone else. He loved me just the way I was; imperfect yet perfect for him.

My only wish is that I would have met him in another lifetime. I'm happy I finally had the opportunity to know what real love feels like, and my search for the impossible became possible.

I played with my life for so long and took it for granted. I allowed men to become the focus of my existence most of my life, and all they did was hurt me.

I could not fully give myself to another man after Ramon because they were not worthy of me, or my love. I realized I am the prize, and I refuse to subject myself to anyone who doesn't recognize that.

I will not settle for just anyone again. I am no longer desperate for love. I stopped searching for a man's validation. I realized I was loved before I was conceived in my mother's womb. No one could love me the way God loves me. I decided to let love find me.

I've cried, laughed and loved. I haven't miss out on a thing. Now it's time that I devote myself to the divine entity; a supreme being that died for me, so that I could live. I realized all I need is the love of God to keep me safe, and warm. I don't have to worry about being lied to, cheated on, or abused ever again.

My search is over, and I can rest in peace just knowing that I am loved far beyond what any man can give. I'm loved by my creator, and that is all I need.

Chapter Twenty-Three

Past, Present, and Future

It was the December, 9, 2013; a day I'll painfully remember forever. It was cold, and cloudy outside, and I was sick with the flu when my brother whom I shared a house with burst into my bedroom. He had his cell phone glued to his ear as he rambled something about daddy.

I was highly medicated, and could barely understand the words he was blurting out at me. He said daddy had been in a car accident, and he needed to use my car to pick up mama. I quickly jumped out of bed, and handed him my keys.

I inquired if daddy was ok and he gestured in a manner that lead me to believe everything was fine. I tried to go back to sleep, but I was worried, so after an hour I started to call my brother, but I got no answer. I called mama, still no answer. I started to feel a sense of urgency, and my stomach began to hurt.

I kept calling, and texting for hours then fear begin to take over me. I frantically called my daughters; sisters, and my best friend Alexis because she always had of way of calming me down. She told me to call the local hospital to see if he was there.

I called the emergency room; gave them daddy's name and waited for them to tell me everything was ok. The nurse quickly asked who I was, and when I identified myself. She asked me where I lived, and urged me to come to the hospital right away.

I asked if he was alright, and then there was silence for a few seconds and then she advised me she could not release any information over the phone.

I hung up the phone, and began to run through the house crying; screaming, and hyperventilating. My chest felt heavy; as though someone was standing on it.

Moments later Mama finally called. She spoke in a monotone almost robotic voice and calmly said; "Daddy didn't make it." I threw the phone on the floor, and ran head first into the wall; fell to my knees, and screamed.

Daddy died sudden, and unexpectedly while driving to the gym. He had a massive heart attack and he plowed into our neighbors' fence and he was gone. We had just celebrated his seventy-second birthday that November. We had just spent Thanksgiving together. Daddy beat prostate cancer, and I just knew he was invincible.

My sister Tina picked me up, and we both drove to our parents' house in complete silence. The coroner called us the next morning, and said daddy died instantly. His heart just stopped. I felt so lost, and confused. I was frustrated, and angry at myself that he didn't live to see me become the woman that he knew I was inside.

When I walked through the door of the Mortuary, and saw his name in big black letters; tears began to flow, and I felt a lump in my throat. I suddenly began to panic, and I couldn't breathe. I ran to the bathroom, and began to scream at the top of my lungs.

I looked in the mirror, and saw reality. Daddy was gone, and all the crying in the world wasn't going to bring him back. I peered at my reflection, not knowing what to do next. They ushered us into the tiny chapel where my father's body lay in a royal blue casket with the United States flag draped over it.

The top of the casket was open and as everyone walked toward it to view his body for the last time, I stood there frozen; afraid to see his lifeless body.

I walked slowly to the coffin, and my knees began to buckle. I looked inside to see my father lying in the black tuxedo he wore to walk me down the aisle when I got married. I leaned over, and kissed him gently on the forehead. I stood there staring at him waiting for him to open his eyes, and tell me it was a joke; but he didn't.

I walked to the front row, and took a seat next to mama. I never saw mama cry once. She sat there with her head held high as people walked by to show their respect. I heard weeping, and sniffles in the distance, and as the room began to fill; I realized just how loved, and respected my father was.

It hurt me that he'd never have the opportunity to read my book, or see me accomplish my dreams. I wanted him to be proud of me; to know that everything he'd preached wasn't in vain, and that I was no longer a failure.

I was upset at God for taking such a great man away from us so soon. I began to realize life is temporary, and that we're all going to die someday. Daddy did what he had to do on this earth. He gave us his knowledge, and wisdom so that we could become responsible; independent individuals. He did his job, and when it was complete, he had to leave.

I realized I didn't let him down; I let myself down by not being the person God created me to be. Daddy was proud of me no matter what. I know he wanted more for me than he ever had for himself. He loved me despite my poor choices, and bad decisions. Mama lost the love of her life. The man she'd been with since the age of fourteen. The man she'd married at sixteen; created five children with, ten grandchildren, and five great grandchildren. The man who'd loved her from a teenager to his existence as a man came to an end; whom she loved with all her heart, and soul.

I knew mama was in so much pain, yet I could do nothing to help ease her sorrow. All I could do was watched, and cry in shame at myself. Daddy was her soul mate; her rock, and her best friend, and she was his. I'd never known such love, and was sadden that it was taken away from my mother.

The grief she felt consumed me, I could feel her anguish, and her emptiness; yet all she did was smile, and say; "God is good". My mother is the strongest woman I know. She endured so many obstacles, yet she never lost her faith in God.

On Thursday, December, ninetieth-two-thousand-thirteen daddy was laid to rest; in Military fashion. There were members of the United States Navy saluting my father for his service to his country. I sat next to Mama as they folded up the flag, and handed it to her. They did a gun salute, and just as the coordinator announced it was over, I stood to my feet and told him I'd written a poem for my father, and I couldn't leave until I read it. It was titled "Dear Daddy."

I stood before my father's casket, and composed myself the best

I could. I read my poem with such pride, and dignity, like the graduation speech I'd recited in the sixth grade. I said goodbye to the only man in my life that I knew truly loved me no matter what. Instead of feeling abandoned, I felt blessed because unlike so many other children; I had a father for fifty-one years of my life.

Most of my existence I thought I was a good person. I couldn't understand why bad things happened to me. I'd given to the homeless, and helped anyone who was in need, but I did it expecting something in return.

I wanted praise and respect. I didn't know I wasn't doing it from my heart. I realized giving with the expectation of receiving something in return; doesn't make you a good person.

My father was a good man, he practiced what he preached, was humble, and accepted the life he was given. His death gave me a reality check, and it took losing him for me to understand that I was rich with love.

For years my life was a figment of my imagination, and I played the leading role of the victim. I sat back, and watched as life passed me by. I blamed everyone for my failures but me. The life I envisioned for myself; was not the life I'd lived. I resided in a fantasy world, because it was easier to pretend then to face reality.

I'd never gone anywhere, or done anything of any real importance. I'd never been truly loved, and adored by a man the way my mother had been loved by my father. I couldn't come close to being the mother to my children that my mother was to me.

I thought I was a failure as a woman, and every time I looked at my image in the mirror I saw nothing. I gave up my power, and stopped believing in myself. I let every bad circumstance dictate my future. Instead of taking control of my life; I destroyed myself with bad choices over, and over again.

I wanted answers from God, but when I didn't get the answers I wanted; I ignored the truth. I wanted things to be easy. I realized that everyone that loved God suffered; even Jesus. Did I think I was better than Jesus?

I had to stop searching for someone or something to bring me joy; peace, and happiness. I had to learn how to look inside myself; into the depths of my inner soul, and believe that God was all I needed.

I had to stop putting my trust, and faith in people, because most of them were just like me; lying to themselves, and pretending. Life was a big masquerade, and everyone I thought I knew; probably wore a mask to hide who they really were inside just like me.

I understand that life isn't fair or easy. That every day I wake up; I had to fight for what I want, instead of throwing in the towel, and searching for someone to save me.

I remembered all the times daddy tried to warn me about life, but I wouldn't listen. I realized daddy was sharing his reality with me, because he didn't want me to struggle like he had. He saw greatness in me; he saw my strengths, and weaknesses.

At age fifty-two; I started to envision myself as God sees me. I started to recognize the blessings God had given me and not focus on the things I didn't have, or my past mistakes. I was blessed to give life to three wonderful children. They gave me five beautiful grandchildren. I survived molestation; rape, depression, abuse, prison, and even death. I beat alcoholism, and drug addiction; and I continued to exist without a man.

When I remembered all those things; I realized just how much God loved me! He loved me from the time I was conceived in my mother's womb, and he will love me until my body is submerged in a tomb.

He gave me life so that I could do great things; yet I continued to seek things that wasn't in God's plan for my life. I had to ask God for forgiveness, and then I had to learn how to forgive myself, and that's when I began to live!

Every day that I am blessed to wake up; I know there is a purpose for my life. Instead of blaming God, I began trusting God through all the turmoil.

Most of my life I made men, money and material things my God. Instead of praying, and having faith; I cried, and complained. I see the goodness of God, and his unconditional love for me. Anyone can trust God when things are going good, it's when things are going bad that I learned to trust him.

I'd made a mess of my life; but God got me through it. I spent a majority of it in hospitals fighting for my life, Heart Disease, Kidney failure, female problems you name it, the doctor's wrote me off a few times, but that wasn't in God's plan.

I'd spent years mad at God for my terrible life. Accusing everyone, and everything for my failures; because I was the victim.

I never realized that I needed to look in the mirror at the one person who'd made these bad choices. I needed to take ownership of my life, and speak into existence the things I was going to accomplish and not let my past dictate my future.

I was imprisoned in my mind. The words I spoke into the universe were the words that snared my success. The choices I made hurt so many people, and nearly destroyed me. I was my own worst enemy; and didn't even know it!

The course of events that altered my life is my testimony, and I hope that it will inspire, and empower someone else to keep believing in themselves no matter what hurdles they are faced with.

This book is not just about my struggles, but about the victory to overcome obstacles; the wisdom to trust in a higher power, and the faith to believe all things are possible if you believe. Life is about choices; you can choose to do right or wrong; good or evil it's all up to you.

The church taught me that faith without work is dead. You have to do the work to accomplish the things in life that you want. My life had its share of joy; pain, failure, and success. But that's all a part of living.

I found there is a higher power in the universe; one that can carry you through the trenches, and give you happiness and inner peace. I realized that God kept giving me chances, because there was a purpose for my life.

God saw something in me that I didn't see in myself, he saw my heart, and knew I was hungry for love.

Chapter Twenty-Four

Nothing is Too Hard for God

At the ripe young age of fifty-two, I've learned life is not worth living if you don't love, and value yourself. I'm no longer a victim, I'm victorious. I don't need a man to validate me, or my name tattooed on someone's chest to feel special.

I don't need friends to make me feel complete, and I don't need fortune or fame to make me feel accomplished. I am blessed, and highly favored, because I matter to God.

For years I took my life for granted, but now I appreciate just waking up every day. I am thankful for all the wonderful gifts God has given me.

This life is temporary; what people think about you shouldn't matter. What's important is what God thinks of you.

Life's lessons taught me to see beyond what the eyes can see; to believe in myself, and never give up.

I lost my job in January 7, 2013. I was down, and depressed. I didn't know what I was going to do, so I ran to the bottle to ease my pain.

My daughter Monica called me out of the blue, and said "Mama get on your knees, and ask God to show you what he wants you to do."

I did as she instructed, and when I rose to my feet; I put down the bottle, picked up a pen, and started to write.

I wrote twenty-one chapters in three months. I knew then what God wanted me to do.

I enrolled in college to further my education. I joined a gym not just to lose weight, but to become healthy in my body, mind, and spirit.

I take long walks by myself, to smell the roses. I watch the birds

soar across the sky, and appreciate God's creations no matter how big or small.

I spend time with my children, and grandchildren to make memories that I can be proud of. I read inspirational books to lift me up, and give me strength.

I pray as much as I can for God to let me be a light to somebody else who may be going through the same things that I have. I ask forgiveness for my thoughts that may not be pleasing to God. I searched my soul to make sure that when I leave this earth I will die guilt free.

There is no ending to my story, because my journey is just beginning. This is my life, and I plan to live it the way God intended. I claim victory not defeat. I speak abundance not poverty.

Now when I look in the mirror I see a beautiful black Queen, and God is my King. It doesn't matter what I look like on the outside. Beauty fades, but the heart stays the same.

You have to know your worth, and conquer your fears. Don't ever accept failure as an option, and never let anyone break your spirit, or steal your joy.

Let go of all the negative things that are holding you back, and focus on the positive things in your life. Don't take another day that God wakes you up for granted.

Believe God will tip the scales in your favor. Let go of the past, and begin looking forward to a brighter future. I can now look in a mirror, and really be proud of the daughter, women, mother, sister and grandmother staring back at me. I don't have to hide behind makeup, and a fake smile any longer.

I decided there was no more time for me to waste. Yesterday is gone, and I can never get it back. I changed my circumstances because I changed my way of thinking.

I don't focus on what I don't have any more, because there is always someone in a worst situation. I learned to ask God for guidance, and understanding, I've learned to have faith, and not give up just because things don't work out the way I want them too.

When one door closes; another will open. I stopped making people, and material things the center of my life. I learned to love being around myself; doing things alone.

I learned to appreciate every scar; and wrinkle, because they hold memories; some good, and some bad, and they are there for a reason.

I've buried so many of my family, and friends before they ever had a chance to really live. I survived such a wild, and dangerous life. I've been at death's door more times then I care to remember.

The doctors had given up on me numerous times. I'm still here because God's didn't give up on me. He loved me enough to use me as a tool, to share my story, and tell somebody about the goodness of God.

I'm not where I want to be in life, but I'm headed in the right direction. There are evil forces in the universe that try to deceive us into thinking we are limited in the things we can accomplish.

There is a God so powerful, and magnificent, and if we believe we will achieve all the wondrous gifts that are awaiting us. All you need is faith the size of a mustard seed.

Open your heart, and mind to the impossible. Never give up, no matter what you're faced with. Keep believing, and you will see there is nothing too hard for God! As long as you have faith there is hope, and your tests will become your testimony.